Under the Editorship of

John E. Horrocks
The Ohio State University

Houghton Mifflin Company
Boston
NEW YORK
ATLANTA
GENEVA, ILL.
DALLAS
PALO ALTO

CROSS-NATIONAL RESEARCH:

Social-Psychological Methods and Problems

Guy J. Manaster

The University of Texas

Robert J. Havighurst

The University of Chicago

Quotation and test items from adaptations of Dennis's Uses Test, Osgood's Semantic Differential, and Peck's Scoring System from Havighurst, R. J., Dubois, M. E., Csikszentmihalyi, M., and Doll, R. (1965), *A Cross-National Study of Buenos Aires and Chicago Adolescents*, reprinted with permission of the publisher, S. Karger, Basel, Switzerland.

Test items from Havighurst, R. J. and Neugarten, B. L. (1955), *American Indian and White Children* reprinted by permission of The University of Chicago Press. Copyright 1955 by The University of Chicago. All rights reserved. Published 1955. Composed and printed by THE UNIVERSITY OF CHICAGO PRESS, Chicago, Illinois, U.S.A.

Test items from Anderson, H. H. and Anderson, G. L. (1961), "Image of the Teacher by Adolescent Children in Seven Countries" in the *American Journal of Orthopsychiatry*, Vol. 31, pp. 481–492. Copyright, the American Orthopsychiatric Association, Inc. Reproduced by permission.

Test items from Würsten, H. (1960), "Story Completions: Madeleine Thomas Stories and Similar Methods" in *Projective Techniques with Children*, edited by A. I. Rabin and M. R. Haworth, pp. 192–209. By permission of the publisher, Grune & Stratton, Inc.

Printed in U.S.A.
Library of Congress Catalog Card Number: 78-169721
ISBN: 0-395-13472-2

Contents

Editor's Foreword

The ultimate business of the social sciences is to formulate and test theories which explore the nature of man as an individual and as a socialized member of a group. While speculation is usually a beginning step in this enterprise, its implementation depends on research comprised of description, classification, and sometimes experimentation. Unfortunately, research can be parochial. A single sample, particularly when examined in a multivariate naturalistic setting rather than a controlled psychological laboratory, at best provides only a tentative generalization about man as a species. Replication using other samples in various contexts increases the security with which the generalizations can be made; but given the universality of man's presence on the earth and the behavioral variations induced by cultural differences, only limited generalizations can be made even from successive replications within a single national cultural setting.

Of course research need not be confined to sequential repetition in a single culture. Cooperative cross-cultural research can coordinate parallel, often interdisciplinary, efforts by investigators working simultaneously in different cultures. The present interest in cross-cultural and cross-national research is manifested by the growing number of contemporary efforts. These range from highly organized groups of researchers coordinating their work in many cultures, to the less organizationally complex attempts of a cooperating pair from two different countries, and even to the lone investigator who travels to several cultural or national settings to collect his data. One of the more ambitious examples of coordinated cross-national effort is a multidisciplinary study of child development being simultaneously carried on from centers in Brussels, Dakar, Kampala, London, Louisville, Paris, Stockholm, and Zurich. Although each of these centers concentrates on a different aspect of human development, they all follow a predetermined base line of investigation.

The coming decade may well witness significant gains in the number of social scientists engaging in cross-national research. Yet such research of acceptable quality is not easily achieved because of problems of methodology, of language equivalence and translation, of cultural outlook, of national and personal research biases, and of time, cost, and geographical distance— problems not ordinarily encountered in intra-national research. Here especially the instruments and techniques must be uniformly designed to insure that the data are maximally comparable. Approaches ordinarily used by researchers in their own countries are seldom directly exportable even when use of a common language is possible. The result is that cross-national research methodology has become a specialty in its own right, requiring appropriate training and information for those who hope to benefit from it.

The present volume by Professors Manaster and Havighurst is a handbook of how and why to design and perform cross-national research. Although measurement is their primary concern, the authors also include a general discussion of related topics, issues of sample selection, and ways of organizing and implementing a research program. This book is not a theoretical treatise but an explicitly practical compendium of answers that a cross-national researcher must know to accomplish his research. However, *Cross-National Research: Social-Psychological Methods and Problems* is not merely a cookbook. The authors provide a firm factual rationale for each of their suggestions.

Books are so often written from vicarious experience, particularly in technical fields, that it is a pleasure to find one written by two men who can bring such an excellent background of personal achievement to their task; both Havighurst and Manaster speak from the vantage point of direct involvement in cross-national research. It is also particularly appropriate that a methodology book on cross-national research should be written jointly by members of the faculties of the University of Texas and the University of Chicago, two institutions that have long stood at the forefront of cross-national research.

John E. Horrocks

Preface

Cross-national research has expanded tremendously since 1950, principally in the area of social psychology. Researchers have gathered much valuable information by comparing the behavior, beliefs, and attitudes of subgroups within complex societies; the extension of these studies to include groups in more than one country promises to provide even greater insight into the nature of man as a species. These studies are the substance of this book.

Both of us have been interested in cross-national research for some time, and we have actively participated together in one major project, the Study of Coping Behavior of Children and Adolescents. This seven nation study was conceived at the Conference on Cross-National Research at the University of Chicago in 1964, with the financial support of the United States Office of Education. Out of this conference developed a nucleus of researchers, with Robert F. Peck of the University of Texas as the central figure. Much of the concrete illustrative material in this book is derived from our experience in that study.

Guy Manaster worked as field director in the Chicago Station of the Research on Coping Behavior and collaborated with international colleagues in the development of research instruments and their validation with cross-national data. He also undertook research with graduate students at the University of Puerto Rico to accumulate data relevant to the already completed Buenos Aires-Chicago Study.

Robert Havighurst first became interested in cross-national research when he taught at the Canterbury University in New Zealand and supervised graduate students whose work on child development could be compared with studies made in the United States. He followed this experience with a period of several years in South America, chiefly in Brazil and Argentina, where he worked with Latin American colleagues on social-psychological studies. In 1961 while teaching at the University of Buenos Aires he organized research on adolescents which he later replicated in Chicago.

This book, then, represents experience with a number of cross-national investigations that brought us into contact with many of the problems of cross-national social psychological research. Our aim is to present these problems and often their possible solution, as practical aids to other researchers, especially young people who are just entering this interesting and complex area of work.

This book is based, to a great degree on experience, experience which did not have the benefit of a book of this sort. In 1969 Coleman wrote: "There has not appeared a literature on the specific methodological problems of cross-national surveys; it is clear that one is coming to be needed." We hope this volume fills that gap.

We are indebted to our colleagues in the cross-national studies for what we have learned from them. We also wish to acknowledge the intelligent and devoted technical assistance of our wives, Jane Manaster and Edythe Havighurst, in the analysis of data and the preparation of the manuscript.

Guy J. Manaster
Robert J. Havighurst

CROSS-NATIONAL RESEARCH: SOCIAL-PSYCHOLOGICAL METHODS AND PROBLEMS

General Introduction

THE COMPARISON OF PEOPLE from different nations or different cultural groups has become an important part of behavioral science in recent years. The goal of these comparative studies is to discover and explain differences of behavior and development among human beings and thus to achieve a deeper understanding of man as a species.

Cross-national comparisons are one form of cross-cultural comparison. If we use the simple definition of a culture as a common set of learned behaviors and beliefs, we can see that a group of adolescents in Chicago, for example, can represent several cultures. They represent the culture of the United States of America, the culture of their sex group, the culture of their social-class group, and the culture of their age group. Thus, national culture is only one of a number of influences determining how people behave and believe.

Devereux, Bronfenbrenner, and Suci (1962, p. 488) introduce their cross-national study by outlining the opportunities and problems inherent in this type of research:

> Cross-national comparisons represent for the social scientist a combination of challenging opportunities and of tricky methodological pitfalls. The opportunities lie in the chance such comparisons provide of shaking hypotheses free from particular sets of cultural entanglements and for catching strategic variables in new ranges and combinations. The pitfalls lie not only in the problems to be faced in the cross-national translation of variables, but also in the fact that most such comparisons involve the reconciliation of basically non-comparable data, gathered by diverse investigations with diverse methods and for diverse purposes.

The purpose of this book is to make the opportunities of cross-national research more accessible by discussing problems inherent in defining, organizing, and implementing such research.

As we report numerous studies in this book, finding fault with many, we reaffirm our faith in the potential of cross-national research. "Shaking hypotheses free from particular sets of cultural entanglements" is in part the result of "catching strategic variables in new ranges and combinations" (Devereux *et al.* 1962). But in cross-national work we find responses, variables, patterns, etc., which do not fit our existing notions and theories. Studies may lack breadth in theory or method and yet generate new theory, new method, and new data. Building a case for the generation of new data by means of psychological naturalism in cross-cultural studies, Gutmann (1969, p. 163) states:

> We are most likely to stimulate new attention and to generate new kinds of data by stepping out of accustomed action frameworks, and by waiting for unexpected regularities to announce themselves. Then the agents implicated in these inferred regularities, and the events that summate to them become, more and more explicitly, our data. We have not declared in advance what the data should be; rather, in our experience, it has forced itself on our attention. In effect, we create data by stepping out of our accustomed ecologies, and by changing our relation to them.

The social sciences abound in theory and knowledge emanating from unexpected cross-national experience.

Definition of "Cross-National" Research

Today sociologists, anthropologists, psychologists, and psychiatrists are doing research in their own fields or in such interdisciplinary areas as social anthropology which they call transcultural, cross-cultural, or cross-national. Educators do equivalent research under the main heading of comparative education. Sometimes gross differences exist in the methods and in the aims of these variously labeled studies. Often the same method is applied to studies with different aims; in these cases the perspective from which the data are analyzed and discussed determines the label.

In this book we will focus discussion on cross-national social-psychological research, its problems and its methods. Cross-national social-psychological research is any investigation of individual and group differences within and between psychological and sociological variables which is carried out in more than one country or culture. The variable "country" makes the study cross-national; and since countries differ to greater or lesser extents in their basic culture, cross-national studies are often referred to as cross-cultural studies. We prefer to differentiate cross-national social-psychological research from cross-cultural research.

The Extent of Cultural Differences

Any two modern nationality groups differ completely in few behaviors or beliefs. We expect their members to speak different languages and to play different forms of sports, such as football and soccer; but in most areas of behavior and belief we expect them to be similar. What differences do exist will generally register only as a few points on the social-psychological instruments used to explore differences between two groups.

Certain factors within the organism and within human society tend to make all members of the human race alike in some ways of behaving and believing. This likeness among human beings means that various subcultures produce relatively small cultural variations. The factors which contribute heavily to the similarities among all human beings include:

1. *Biological drives.* The hunger drive leads to common behavior and attitudes about food. The sex drive leads to common behavior and general attitudes about sex. The existence of two sexes leads to sex roles which are to some extent common among all human societies, although considerable differences exist among cultural groups, especially among primitive societies.

2. *Mental maturation.* The biological growth of the nervous system and the cognitive growth of the mind provide the basis for speaking, counting, reading, reasoning, and other cognitive functions. Except for language differences, the differences between modern societies in mental development are relatively small.

Factors which tend to produce even greater behavioral similarities among some groups of twentieth century human beings include:

1   *The experience of growing up in a family.* The child learns a set of attitudes and expectations about fathers, mothers, relations to adult authority, relations with siblings and other kin. Although the family experience varies somewhat from one cultural group to another, these differences are small compared with the broad similarities found among societies at the same general level of social evolution.

2   *The experience of growing up in a certain social class.* The existence of a social structure based largely on occupational differentiation gives all people common perceptions of society and of the occupational and personal characteristics that determine status in that society. The membership of a person in a particular social class then gives him certain attitudes toward education, property, family relations, and certain occupational aspirations that he shares with people of similar social class in other societies.

3   *Living in an urban-industrial society.* For people who have grown up in a twentieth century urban-industrial society, many common experiences lead to common ways of behaving and believing. Attitudes toward school, education, and teachers are likely to be similar; common habits and attitudes develop with respect to travel, vacations, weekends, commercial amusements, use of the telephone and other mechanical devices, etc. Consideration of these similarities of human experience leads to the conclusion that cultural differences among the most modern industrial and urban societies are not great. We must examine minor differences.

Intra-cultural Variability. Certain factors within the organism and within the social group tend to make all members of a given social group different from one another in some ways of behaving and believing. They inherit different combinations of genes (except for the rare cases of identical twins), and they are treated differently within their families, their play groups, and their schools. Therefore we should expect to find a large amount of intra-group or individual variability in the characteristics we try to measure. The differences *within* a subcultural group are likely to be large compared with the differences between subcultural groups.

Generally speaking, two cultural groups differ in average score on a social-psychological test, but they differ very little in range of scores or in the shape of the distribution of scores. Therefore we tend to compare averages and not standard deviations or ranges, although comparisons of standard deviations would probably show some interesting cultural differences and should be made more frequently.

Other Types of Cultural Differences.   Other types of behavior are not normally distributed in any cultural group, and these behaviors differentiate the groups. One of these is a behavior or a belief customary in one society and absent or rare in another, for example, a set of religious beliefs and practices. Jewish religious beliefs are quite universal among Jews, Muslim beliefs among Muslims, and Roman Catholic beliefs among Catholics. We distinguish the group by its religion.

Another example is eating rice, a behavior which is common among many national groups, while eating potatoes is common among contrasting groups. In this example, the frequency of rice-eating or potato-eating is represented by a J-curve, with a very high proportion eating rice or potatoes regularly, and decreasing proportions of the population eating rice or potatoes less frequently. Speaking English has a similar distribution among residents of the USA. An example in the area of attitudes, is support of the free enterprise system of economic activity. This variable would show a J-curve distribution in the USA, if it were measured in terms of intensity and coverage of various types of common activity; in the Soviet Union a similar J-curve would characterize support of a socialistic system of economy.

Other types of behavior that vary among cultural groups and do not have a normal distribution occur rarely in some cultural groups and not at all in others. For example, a favorable attitude toward civil disobedience to laws which are considered unjust is found only rarely, and primarily in the few countries with a tradition of democracy. Another example is the act of suicide as atonement for failure to complete an important and expected task, as in the occasional practice of *hara-kiri* among the Japanese.

Normally Distributed Behaviors and Attitudes. While cultural differences are important to an understanding of human societies the social psychologist has directed his attention primarily toward behaviors and attitudes which are present in all or nearly all social groups, behaviors which can be measured in terms of frequency or intensity and which have a quasi-normal distribution in most social groups. The difference between social groups, then, appears in the mean scores on measuring instruments and sometimes in the distribution or standard deviation of the scores.

The question social scientists ask is: Are social and psychological differences between one social group and another objectively measurable? We believe such differences exist but have not yet been adequately identified and measured. To illustrate the problem, let us assume that we wish to compare a group of Chicago teen-agers with a group of Buenos Aires teen-agers on attitudes toward urban living, social change, and traditions. We construct an attitude test to measure what we call *Modernism.* We can be certain that the members of the two national samples will vary greatly in their scores on this test. We can also hypothesize that the two national samples will differ in mean scores on the test. We must realize that much of the variance of scores on the tests will be *among individuals* in the two groups, and only a small part of the variance will exist *between the two national groups.*

Suppose we establish the fact that a statistically reliable difference exists between the Chicago and Buenos Aires samples. Before we can draw the conclusion that the difference is a result of growing up in different national cultures, we must examine our samples more carefully.

The Chicago sample contains boys and girls from several schools, and the Buenos Aires sample contains boys and girls from several schools. Do the two samples come from the same social classes in the same proportions? If not, then the difference between the two samples may be due to differences between social-class groups rather than differences between nationality groups.

Also, boys' attitudes about *Modernism* may differ from girls' and therefore we must know whether proportions of boys in the two samples were equal. Then age differences between the two samples may exist. If so, we may be seeing differences between two age-group cultures rather than between two national groups.

Finally, the Buenos Aires group may be largely Catholic while the Chicago group is largely Protestant. If so, perhaps the difference we note between the two groups is a difference between religious cultures rather than a difference between national cultures.

Our technical problem in looking for differences between national cultures is to control our samples for other cultural factors which may produce differences in social attitudes. We must try to answer the questions:

1 What differences exist between the two national groups?

2 How do these national differences compare in size and nature with differences between sexes, social classes, age groups, and religious groups?

Methods of Studying Cultural Differences

If we use social-psychological tests to study differences between cultural groups, the tests must be selected and their results interpreted with considerable sophistication, based on knowledge of cultural differences and how they arise. Twenty or thirty years ago, tests of ability, intelligence, and personality were applied to various cultural groups with the naive expectation that these tests could be interpreted in exactly the same way that they were interpreted in the countries or societies where they were developed and validated. Thus, European and North American intelligence tests of the performance type were administered to African people, and their low results were taken to indicate inferior intelligence. The dubious quality of the interpretations was made clear when projective tests were applied to people of alien cultures. For example, a study of North African Moroccans with the Rorschach Test found that the usual patterns of Moroccan responses were similar to the abnormal patterns given by neurotic individuals in the United States and North Europe (Bleuler and Bleuler 1935). Several such experiences convinced psychologists that they must take culture into account when giving and interpreting psychological tests.

Taking culture into account is not easy, but it is possible, as has been shown by a number of psychologists who understand cultural anthropology. Each new cultural group creates a new problem of test administration and interpretation. This is just as true of a new social-class group or age group as it is of a new national group.

Causes of Differences Between Groups in Test Performance

The differences between groups of people in their performance on psychological tests *may* be due to the following factors:

> *Biological differences.* If intelligence, artistic talent, personality qualities, and other psychological qualities are systematically related to social and racial groups in the way that skin color, hair, height, eye color, etc., are related to such groups, then the superiority or inferiority of a group of people is likely to be interpreted as due to anatomical qualities which they possess. However, no evidence suggests that social or racial groups possess biological qualities which differentiate their performance on psychological tests. But such differences between the sexes may exist.

> *Cultural Differences.* Cultural groups are likely to differ as groups on many psychological tests because they differ systematically from one another in one or more of the following respects:

> *Experience with the stimulus—the content of the test or instrument.* The Rorschach ink blot test may be much more strange to people of one cultural group than to people of another. The vocabulary items of an intelligence test may be more familiar to people of one social class than of another. And a simple translation of the items of an English vocabulary test into Spanish may result in a test with a quite different degree of difficulty for Spanish-speaking subjects, because the words used in the translation may not have the same degree of "difficulty" as the words in the original test. Various cultural groups may also have varying degrees of experience with an interview and with an interviewer. People of one

culture may tell more of what they know or believe to a stranger in an interview than people of another culture.

Motivation with respect to the test. Few tests or psychological instruments yield useful data if the subject does not cooperate with the test administrator. An individual intelligence test is often better than a group test because the administrator of an individual test can encourage the individual taking the test. In some of the simpler societies competitive spirit among the children is not encouraged. They are taught to be cooperative, and they carry this spirit into their school work; when they are called upon to compete with other children in a test situation, they may not exert themselves. This is an important factor in establishing comparative studies of school achievement. However, it does not interfere particularly with performance on a test of personality or attitudes where competition is not involved. On a test of intelligence or achievement, people who do not expect the test to help them may not do their best. For this reason, children of lower-class families and of cultural groups which have been denied opportunity are likely to do less well on such tests than they would do if they were strongly motivated.

Experience with language. Most tests require the use of language; the respondent's understanding of the language of the test and his own use of language in the test are therefore crucial elements.

Language is an extremely complex element of culture. Some cultural groups, notably the upper-middle class of North America and North Europe, systematically train their children to use language in a rational, orderly way, related to the purpose they have in mind—to prove something, to describe a happening, to express an emotion, or to give a direction. Other cultural groups use language more loosely, with less logical structure and with less clear-cut meaning.

Another cultural difference between groups is the different meanings they assign to some commonly-used expressions. Thus, when a waitress in a restaurant in the southern part of North America addresses her customer as "honey," her meaning may be the same as that of another waitress in a northern state who addresses him as "sir." These differences may interfere with the interpretation of results on an attitude questionnaire, where a given word may have a more favorable connotation for one cultural group than for another.

Cultural differences in developmental experience. The major differences between groups which can be registered and measured with psychological instruments are differences due to developmental experiences which are part of the culture. Thus, the social expectations for behavior appropriate to a young man are different from those for a young woman, and these differences vary from one culture to another. The varied training received by children across cultural groups is another factor.

Interaction of the four types of cultural effect. The actual performance of an individual on a psychological test is the result of interaction of all four of these factors. Our goal is to separate out the effects of cultural differences in developmental experience from the other effects, controlling these others, keeping them constant if possible or reducing them to an accountable minimum.

This task is not easy. The experimenter cannot remove the effects of experience with the stimulus, of motivation, and of language usage. Thus no test is "culture-free"; no test can be presented to people of various cultures in such a way that their performance is not affected by these three cultural elements. The attempt to create a "culture-common test" or instrument is generally made by psychologists who understand something about cultural differences. The characteristics of such an instrument are: 1) it draws upon aspects of cultural experience which are common to all people taking the test—for example, language, family situations, common objects in the everyday experience, and number systems which all hold in common;

2) it is designed to have about equal degrees of intrinsic interest for the different cultural groups who will use it; 3) it uses a form of language which is widely familiar, and the directions are stated in simple, operational terms.

Varieties of Cross-National Studies

The cross-national or cross-cultural studies in which we are interested for the purposes of this book follow three general designs.

Studies within a complex society. It might be useful to compare a number of subcultures within the USA or another complex society, for example regional differences, or differences between groups of different skin color, or between ethnic subgroups such as Japanese-Americans, Negroes, Mexican-Americans, Puerto Ricans, Cubans, and American Indians. Among American Indians one might study differences between tribal groups.

Studies of differences between two well-defined national groups. This is the simplest type of study, conceptually, though it may be quite complicated to accomplish. Many investigators compare an American group on which they have test data with a group from another country, without taking care to make their American sample or their other national sample truly representative of the national cultures that are supposedly being compared.

Studies of differences among a group of countries. In this kind of study diverse countries are chosen to obtain a wide variety of national cultures. Substantial resources are necessary, resources which have been made available recently by the U. S. Office of Education. For example, the International Study of Achievement in Arithmetic involved cooperation of teams of researchers in a number of countries, together with coordination of their work by a central research office. The Cross-National Study of Coping Behavior involves teams of researchers in seven countries, with a coordinating office at the University of Texas. In ambitious and complex researches of this kind, the first importance is to control all of the subcultural factors which might account for group differences that are not true national cultural differences. That is, the samples which are studied should be identical in sex, age, and social class. If they differ in skin color, or religion, or in other possibly significant ways, these differences, as well as purely national cultural factors, should be kept in clear sight as possible sources of the observed differences in test scores.

Hundreds of studies fit our definition of a cross-national study. They are published in journals of the social sciences and bulletins of national and international agencies and research organizations. The following list of titles of fifty studies spanning the last forty years dramatically illustrates the breath of the field, although not all employ instruments discussed in this book. Some of the studies are quite well-known; many deal with unique topics and methods of inquiry. The list covers many of the cross-national areas of study but not all. The list of titles illustrates Roger Brown's negative response to the following question: "Can one abstract from the list of topics that are being successfully studied in a social-psychological manner the logical class of topics that *should* be studied in this manner and so identify the proper domain of social psychology and foresee its future development?" (Brown 1965)

> The Rio Grande Flood: A comparative study of border communities in disaster
>
> Timing patterns in the development of sexual intimacy: An attitudinal report on three modern Western societies
>
> A cross-cultural study of film preferences on an Indian student population
>
> Compatriot and foreigner: A study of impression formation in three countries
>
> The fitness of names to drawings: A cross-cultural study in Tanganyika
>
> The meanings of leisure
>
> Comparison of nurturance and independence training in Jamaica and Puerto Rico, with consideration of the resulting personality structure and transplanted social patterns

Childhood experiences and adult personality: A cross-cultural study using the concept of ego strength

Social status of the aged in three Indian villages

Some correlates of beliefs in the malevolence and benevolence of supernatural beings: A cross-cultural study

Racial comparisons of ability in immediate recall of logical and nonsense material

Cognitive control in children of Mexico and the U. S. A.

A comparative study of children's play in America and Japan

Stuttering and social structure in two Pacific societies

Nationality and Conformity

A cross-cultural study of anxiety among American and English school children

Personality in Faces: A cross-cultural comparison of impressions of physiognomy and personality in faces

Sex of the communicator as a variable in source credibility

Value orientation, role conflict, and alienation from work: A cross-cultural study

The cross-cultural fruit-tree study

Extremeness, indifference and moderation response sets: A cross-cultural study

Generalized ethnic attitudes in the Arab Near East

The deprived and the privileged: Personality development in English society

Relative neurotic tendency of Chinese and American students

Differences between Chinese and American reactions to the Bernreuter personality inventory

A level-of-aspiration study among the Ramah-Navaho

Some comparative data on class consciousness in Sweden and France

Personality differences between a Hindu and an American group

To be or not to be: A study in suicide

Gestural behavior and social setting

Primary social attitudes: A comparison of attitude patterns in England, Germany and Sweden

Arab-American differences in the judgments of written messages

Some effects of overseas duty on the attitudes of American troops toward host populations

65 and over in Midwest, Kansas, and Yoredale, England

Finnish children's reactions to frustration in the Rosenzweig Test: An ethnic and cultural comparison

A Szondi study of developmental and cultural factors in personality: The seven-year-old

The latency stage story performances of American and Finnish children

Ecological factors in the WAIS Picture Completion Test

Social perceptions in Russian displaced persons and an American comparison group

Assessment of abstract behavior in a non-Western society

National preferences of university students from 23 countries

Moral values across cultures

A Marathi revision of the S.R.A. Youth Inventory

A cross-cultural study of structured groups with unpopular central members

Ethnicity, social class, and adolescent independence from parental control

National stereotypes and foreign contacts

Differences in personality adjustment among different generations of American Jews and non-Jews

Sociocultural factors in responses to stressful life situations: The behavior of aged amputees as an example

The multinational comparative time budget research project: A venture in international research cooperation

Preoccupation with competitiveness and social acceptance among American and English students

Structure of This Book

In Part I of this book, we will discuss the problems of using social-psychological instruments for cross-cultural comparisons —problems of translation from one language or dialect to another, and problems of cross-validation of findings from one research instrument with findings from other instruments.

In the main body (Part II) of this book we shall discuss a number of types of research instruments that can be used in cross-cultural studies—their uses, their strengths, and their difficulties.

Finally, in Part III, we will discuss the practical problems of designing cross-national studies—organizing for cooperation among the various teams in the study, choosing subgroups for comparison, obtaining comparable samples, and problems of administering this kind of research program.

Part One

Problems of Method in the Choice and Preparation of Instruments

Chapter 1

Preparation of Instruments

EVERY ISSUE, EVERY STEP, in cross-national research presents the usual problems of all research and in addition to these the specific problems that working in two or more cultures creates. We will speak in the next chapters about selection of instruments and therein allude to numerous problems of translation and equivalence. In this chapter, we will discuss these problems more generally and touch on a number of other issues which compound the difficulties of selecting and preparing instruments for cross-national research.

Stimulus Equivalence and Language

Whenever respondents are required to answer questions the investigator must attempt to phrase the question so that the respondent understands it. The same question may have to be phrased quite differently if put to people of different ages or socioeconomic backgrounds, in order for them to understand the question—and, most important, understand it the same way.

In designing instruments for use across cultures the language differences draw attention to issues which must be dealt with. Assuming the instrument to be used has met the criteria for use in this type of research the translation procedure is an obvious first step. This procedure can be elaborate and costly.

The most common and simple method for checking translations of social psychological instruments in different languages is "back translation." This method consists of two translations, one from the original language into the second language, and then another translation (by another translator) *back* into the original language. The assumption is, if the "back" translation is the same as the original, then the second language form is the same.

A more elaborate (and costly) scheme which further assures comparability would include the following:

1   "Back translation" by two or more translators at both steps doing the initial translations independently and then working together to perfect their translation.

2   A testing program in which subjects interpret the instrument questions or items, i.e., say what they think the questions ask and mean.

3   Repeating this procedure until the subjects understand the items in the same way as the professionals who administer the tests understand the items.

The most simple, and most important, issue in translations is that respondents in each culture understand the questions in the same way. Certainly this means that the instrument should be in language that is appropriate for the age, socio-economic class and area (dialect) of the respondents.

In many formal and informal ways language conveys attitudes ranging from politeness to easy familiarity. This is of great importance in some cultures and languages and of lesser importance in others. Colloquialisms and simple usages, are often used within a culture to make items more easily understandable. However, caution in translating is required for two reasons: (1) the "special" meanings of the usages cannot, or may not, be translatable, and, (2) their social meanings, on a politeness–familiarity scale, may be quite different. "Do you dig your Dad?" and "Do you like your father?" both ask for an evaluation of the subject's feelings about his father. They ask the same question. But the degree of familiarity in the first question and the directness and seriousness of the second question would no doubt elicit different types of responses. The first question translated into another language and then back translated could well become the second. The question would not be the same in both countries.

Holtzman discussed this problem saying, "semantic value of

particular words and phrases may still differ appreciably across two cultures, leading to different response sets and interpretations of meaning" (Holtzman 1965, p. 74). He uses studies by Peck and Diaz Guerrero (1963), which deal with differential meaning across cultures of the words "love" and "respect," to illustrate how exact translations do not necessarily carry "semantic equivalence." He also illustrates the "confounding of language differences and personality" in "the interesting study reported by Ervin," which raised the question, "Does an individual's personality look noticeably different when expressed in one language rather than in another?" (Holtzman 1965, pp. 74–75)

An example of the variety and practicality of the problem of semantic equivalence is illustrated in Dr. Shunichi Kubo's (1969) memo to colleagues with whom he works on a number of cross-national studies. He mentions some of the linguistic differences which have caused him difficulty in translating instruments originally in English or European languages into Japanese. Among these are: word order differs; particles stand after nouns and resemble English prepositions in usage; sentences often do not or cannot have a subject; specifying number and gender of nouns, adjectives, and verbs in written Japanese is complicated if not impossible; and, the language commonly uses honorifics (what we have referred to as politeness–familiarity scale) "whose complexity would be far beyond any foreigner's imagination."

This discussion has primarily focused on semantic equivalence or the problem of stimulus equivalence when the stimulus is words. The equivalence of nonverbal stimuli, such as in projective techniques or sensory measures, is equally important and involved, as will be seen in the discussion of these types of measures.

Reliability

"The problem of scoring reliability is the problem of agreement on what the data *are*. The problem of validity is the problem of what the data *indicate*" (Brown 1965, p. 438). In the next sections we discuss the particular problems of reliability and validity as they relate to cross-national research. Essentially there are two types of reliability. One is that of the instrument itself, the items that make up the instrument, in order to produce the same results with different parts of a test or over time. The other is that of the scoring procedure to ascertain that the data are interpreted and scored in a consistent manner, according to some defined theory or scale.

Scoring reliability varies from machine scoring, which is highly reliable, to ratings by judges based on interviews and observations and free response tests, which may be greatly unreliable. The section on scorer reliability is especially important for cross-national studies in which the research staff comes from different cultures or countries. An example of reliability on interview rating is given in the discussion of that instrument. Several alternative forms of quantitative computation of reliability coefficients are suggested.

Reliability Between Scorers

Numerous kinds of reliabilities tested in psychological and social psychological studies measure agreement between tests, forms, items, or agreement over time between the same or similar tests, forms, or items. Cronbach (1960, p. 126) says "reliability always refers to consistency throughout a series of measurements." Scorer, or interscorer, reliability refers to consistency through a series of measurements by different measurers. Scorer reliability is not an issue with objective tests but it is crucial with free response instruments such as projective and semiprojective tests and interviews. The issue is raised, and scorer reliability gauged when instruments of this type are employed.

In cross-national or multistation research the issue becomes more complicated. However, a cautious and complete approach to the issue can make the scorer reliability procedure valuable in this type of research. Familiarity with the variety of communication difficulties encountered even in a tight research carried out in one place predicts the potential for chaos in a cross-national study. The purpose of this section is to present a scheme for collecting and analyzing scorer reliability in a cross-national study which will lessen the "potential for chaos."

Scorer reliability assesses whether an instrument is eliciting information which can be rated by scales which are sufficiently well defined to allow many scorers "consistently" to score the same information the same way. This is more than one would normally expect from a scorer reliability test. But a low reliability between scorers does not necessarily mean that they as individuals have not mastered a scoring system. It may mean the instrument is not eliciting scoreable information. The information may not be scoreable due to deficits in the scoring or scaling systems. If all this information is available from this procedure, the following plan is presented to enable the cross-national researcher to pinpoint the fault. This scheme is applicable to complex multistation cooperative research but adaptable to fit the requirements of less ambitious studies.

The scene for the reliability test is set with a number of research centers, having collected data with a free-response instrument, prepared to score the data according to a rating manual or a set of scales. There may be one or more scorers in a station. If the sample (as well as the budget) is large, there will probably be more than one scorer. The scheme we will present will assume the preferable alternative of more than one scorer. It will also be presented without regard to the statistical requirements of sample size or suggestions for the use of statistical techniques all of which depend on the particulars of the study. The organization of the study includes a central station where all data is eventually sent, analyses performed, and from which reports and issues emanate.

Step 1. Intrastation Scorer Reliability

A. The scorers within a station, having thoroughly discussed and familiarized themselves with the scoring system, independently score a subsample of randomly selected instruments. (If the sample at a station represents different subgroups, and, a variety of testers, interviewers and administration conditions, the subsample should by its size or through sampling methods represent the variety in the sample.)

B. The level of reliability within the station is statistically determined for the group of scorers, each scorer against at least one other scorer, and for the subgroups and different test situations. If the reliability levels are not acceptable, the reasons should be determined. If the problems, such as difference of opinion or understanding among scorers, can be remedied, another reliability test should be performed. The results of the reliability test, the individual scorer's ratings, comments on large discrepancies between scorers or between subgroups, and copies of the original instruments should be sent to the central station.

Step 2. First Analysis of Intrastation Reliability Data

A. At the central station an analysis of the reliability data from the several centers leads to the preliminary determination of whether the instrument, scales, and scorers are effective. The following questions can be asked:

1 Is the instrument eliciting scoreable data? Check the number of no answer, don't know, and unscoreable responses.

2 Is the instrument eliciting scoreable data in all subsamples? Check by subsample and categories of test administration and by administrator.

3 Are the scales well defined and understandable? Refer to the level of scorer reliability in each center.

4 Are the scales sufficiently discriminating? Refer to the frequency distribution, the range or spread, on each scale in each center. It should be noted here that it is much easier to get high interscorer reliability if many or all subjects receive the same rating, or the range is small.

5 Are all scorers in all stations consistent in their scoring? Check the individual reliability comparisons.

6 What else might be the problem? Compare the comments from the centers for some consensus as to the specific difficulties.

B. At this point, some previous decisions may be altered in which case rescoring of already collected or new data may be necessary and another intrastation reliability test run. If the intrastation data is judged acceptable, the interstation analysis can begin.

Step 3. Interstation scorer reliability

A. From the sample of instruments used in the interstation reliability test and sent to the central station, equal numbers of instruments from each center, selected for variety of subgroup and quality, are chosen to form a set of instruments representative of all centers. This set of instruments is reproduced and sent to all centers to be scored.

B. The same statistical procedures, analysis, and description of difficulties as outlined in Step I, Part B should be performed and sent to the central station.

Step 4. Analysis of Interstation Reliability Data

A. The analysis of the interstation data begins with a statistical analysis of reliability between scorers across centers, and an overall level of reliability determined. Should this level be found acceptable, a memorandum of congratulations to all centers is in order. However, this pleasure should not be expected.

A more detailed analysis follows by center, by scorer, and by blocks of instruments from each center included in the total set of instruments involved in this test. These analyses should answer, at least, the following questions:

1 Since the reliability within each center on this set of instruments has been determined, which centers agree and which disagree?

2 Which scales or portions of the manual are unreliable, and why? Check both the statistical data and the comments from each center.

3 Is the lower reliability related to the quality of the data? Are the data from some stations scored more inconsistently by some stations? By checking the reliability for the instruments from each center, the comments on problems of scoring, and comparing the quality of the data, some insight into this problem should be gained.

4 Is there at least one scorer at each center whose scores approach a reasonable level?

This complex scheme involves a great deal of work. But for cross-national research purposes advantages to putting the required effort in this procedure are numerous.

The major objection to the scheme is inefficiency in the duplication, or triplication, of effort. Intrastation or interstation testing may seem sufficient. But in cross-national research problems arise which make using both tests advisable; communication between and within centers may result in the unequal distribution of information among all researchers; imprecise definitions and meanings, language and cultural differences complicate matters further. These definitional problems may influence the quality of the data (on an interview, the instruction "active probing" may elicit quite different behavior from a New York interviewer and a Mexican interviewer) or the interpretation of the scales (for example, a situation that may seem frustrating to a German researcher may not seem so to a Brazilian). Problems may arise because of differences in personnel at the various stations, i.e., one station may be staffed by two Ph.D.s and two candidates, while in another the principal investigator is a college student with two secretaries. Problems arise from the differences in the use of language, the quality and quantity of language used by the respondent, which may have different meanings in different cultures. Nuances and true meanings of words may be lost in translation so that a translated instrument would be scored differently than would the test in the original language.

For these reasons and others the scheme is complex. Step I, intrastation test, trains the scorers and build a consensus in each station. If no agreement can be reached within stations, the problem lies in the scales. If some subsamples of instruments agree but not others, error may lie in administrative inconsistencies or in the diversity within the sample. But where agreement is reached within each station regardless of the results that follow in the interstation test, results are analyzable by comparing the basic assumptions and differences between the centers.

Step III, interstation test, covers much of the same ground as the intrastation test, but scoring the data adds the confounding elements of cultural differences, translation, etc. If this test is applied without the previous application of the intrastation test, it is difficult to determine where the problems lie. Each station attempts to reach an acceptable level of reliability on the intrastation test, indicating a certain basic level of understanding when dealing with the data they know best. The interstation test helps locate the differences between stations, and instrument quality, and in what way the quality differs, thereby confusing the reliability issue, and, indicates which (if any) scorer at a station comes closest to agreeing with the cross-national consensus.

The two kinds of analyses enable us to evaluate, at least in part, the following issues:

1   Intrastation Test
    Instrument efficacy
    Instrument efficacy by subsample
    Individual Scorer Reliability (local data)
    Intrastation reliability (local data)
    Scoring method efficacy (local data)

2   Interstation Test
    Individual scorer reliability (combined data)
    Interstation reliability (combined data)
    Scoring method efficacy (across centers)
    Station differences by scale
    Station differences by source of data

With this system it should be possible to evaluate the quality of instrument and data, to establish scorer reliability to a level that permits production scoring, and to understand whatever differences may remain between centers. It is hoped that the use of this scheme will facilitate productive, understandable cross-national results.

Reliability of Instruments

The problem of instrument reliability is inconsistency and instability of response. Historically, three methods are used to estimate the reliability of instruments: split-half, alternate forms, and retest. They have been refined and elaborated and are still the preferred methods. As in all cross-national procedures the usual cautions prevail. In this section we will report the special considerations necessary in reliability work on nonprojective instruments in cross-national research by analyzing the three methods, and will discuss the special problems of reliability of projective type instruments.

Split Half

The "split-half" reliability method is a test of internal consistency, such as the degree of agreement between two halves of the same test. The assumption made in applying this method is that the halves are composed of items of equal difficulty which by virtue of their order in the test or the time allotted to the administration have been given equal attention by the subjects.

When dealing with two or more cultures which may have been chosen for presumably great differences on the variables being investigated, one can expect that items will vary in difficulty across cultures. Certainly on attitude or value measuring instruments an item which presents an accepted statement in one culture may be easy to respond to in another because it is strongly rejected. But in a third culture this same item may prove very difficult because the issue has never been raised. Even in cultures where the items seem equally difficult, they may prove to be of varying difficulty across cultures because of developmental differences in confronting the issues or because of social class differences in relevance.

If an instrument is split according to standards developed in one culture and high reliability is calculated within that country, there is no real reason to believe that the same split will work as well in another country. One way to avoid this problem is to make appropriate splits in each culture, thereby running internal reliability tests within each culture. If in each culture the test is composed of items with the same difficulty overall (even though each item does not have equal difficulty across cultures), an odd-even split or even a random splitting of the instrument could produce a legitimate measure of internal reliability. In order to assure internal reliability of an instrument in all cultures, the items would have to be reduced to the lowest level of difficulty for all subjects which would, of course, make it meaningless. In any event it is possible that an instrument will not be equally reliable in all subject nations, yet will still be acceptable.

The most disconcerting aspect of the "split-half" method relevant to cross-national work is that what may seem relevant in one culture (including the taking of tests) may not seem so to subjects in another culture. What may seem easy in one country may be difficult for subjects in another. In either event, where a test or a number of items is too difficult the respondents may respond randomly. If the test is marked randomly by all members of a group, the split-half reliability would be high, almost as high as if all subjects marked all items the same way. In cross-national studies, it therefore is possible that split-half reliability alone could indicate a reliable test which later is proven invalid.

Alternate Form

The "alternate form" method has one glaring liability in cross-national studies: the "alternate form" must be developed. The entire translation process must be duplicated. The internal consistency aspect (between forms aspect) of this method is much more tenuous because of the additional errors that translation may present. The retest aspect which should be testing stability is compounded by the same problems. Unless two forms of an instrument are necessary for a study, this method is too expensive and time consuming to use in cross-national studies.

Retest

The "retest" or "test–retest" reliability method has the fewest liabilities for cross-national work and several distinct advantages. The retest method is primarily used to test stability of response over time. Length of time between administrations and the effects of memory must be weighed in planning the testing. An extremely long period between test and retest maximizes the possibilities for real change, thereby decreasing the possibility of high reliability. If personality variables, attitudes, and values are scaled from basic to superficial, the less basic variables would be expected to change more readily over time. Since with this method we are testing the instrument and not the variable, a short time period should produce limited changes of meaningful variables. On the other hand a short test administered twice in a short period of time would be significantly influenced by the variable of memory. People would remember some or much of what they did the first time. If a long test or series of tests is administered twice over a reasonable amount of time (four to eight weeks) an individual's position should not have altered significantly and he should also remember few details of his first performance. Therefore the ability of the instrument to measure the same variables over time is tested.

Guilford (1954, p. 374) says, "A retest coefficient of correlation tells us nothing concerning the internal consistency of a test." A retest coefficient of correlation however does indicate whether overall response is consistent when the test is taken twice. If a test is comprised of two or a number of parts, retest coefficients for each part indicate the consistency of response for each part. But these procedures do not determine internal consistency (as the relation between two halves) of the test.

One advantage of the retest method is that it is possible to calculate the item by item agreement from test to retest, and thus to improve an instrument by eliminating or modifying the items on which the retest consistency of response is low.

There are two reasons why responses of people, especially young people, may lack consistency and stability. One is that the stimulus situation evokes ambivalence which leads to an inconsistent response over time. An extreme example would be for an item such as "I like school". A youngster is likely to respond differently at different times to this statement, depending on momentary contingencies.

Secondly, if the test asks for a more general judgment, such as "Everything considered, I like school," it is difficult for youngsters, and for many adults as well, to take every variable into account. This difficulty factor, when a definitive response to a generality is required, certainly leads to inconsistency of response.

"Item difficulty" is a further variable that is systematically related to consistency of response. Suppose we have an arithmetic test for fourth graders. We give students ample time and expect them to finish the test. On a test-retest, we would expect them to show high consistency on the easy items, and low consistency on the difficult items where guessing plays a larger role. In this situation, on attitude, value, or personality tests, the test constructor must make the statements so clear cut that the attitude of the respondent is not ambiguous. Responses such as, "I like my mother" or "I often talk back to my teacher" are likely to be highly reliable because everyone agrees or disagrees. A reliable item is therefore one where almost everyone agrees or disagrees. This type of item can allow reliable group differences between subcultures; i.e., members of a high socioeconomic status (SES) group may almost unanimously agree whereas members of a low SES group may almost unanimously disagree, while in another culture all may be ambivalent or find an item too difficult.

Overall test-retest reliability of an instrument is likely to be high if the instrument is "easy"—if there is general agreement among the subjects in their responses. But the reliability is likely to be low if the instrument is "difficult"—if the subjects are widely divergent among themselves on their responses. Thus, an item that has poor discriminatory value is likely to be more reliable than an item that has good discriminatory value.

We may have to accept low reliabilities in order to get instruments that spread out respondents. There is, however, no point in keeping items which (a) do not discriminate among subjects or (b) draw so many changed responses that they are not at all reliable.

The test-retest method of estimating instrument reliability is the suggested method is cross-national work, for one can test overall stability, stability of parts, and consistency of individual items, without preparing an alternate form or making assumptions about comparability of parts.

Reliability with Projective Type Instruments

Opinions on when, how, and whether to estimate the reliability of projective instruments run the gamut. Murstein (1965, p. 189) examined the multiple problems of reliability measures for projective techniques and found "that projective techniques have lower reliabilities than multiple-choice paper-and-pencil tests because, in addition to the usual sources of error, they add new ones." Yet, "the basic philosophy that 'conventional' statistics are inapplicable to projective techniques is held to be untenable. Several solutions . . . are used to illustrate this point." Karon (1968, p. 102), after a lengthy treatise on validity and reliability, concludes "that for projective tests, validity coefficients are important and that reliability is largely an irrelevant consideration."

Karon (p. 98) goes on to state that "Temporal consistency . . . cannot be a criterion of the measuring instrument unless it is already known (as is rarely the case) that the characteristic being measured is itself temporally stable." If this criticism were valid, it would hold for all types of instruments, not just projectives. However, all theories of personality consistency and common sense tell us that important variables remain stable over long periods of time. Projective techniques are valuable because they elicit information about basic personality constructs. These constructs, if they are indeed basic and important, should be consistent over time.

If reliability tests are applicable to projectives, as Murstein believes, what advantage do we get from using them in cross-national research? The most glaring reason is to test the instrument applicability. In our discussions of specific projective instruments used in past research, real questions will be raised about their use across cultures. If the projective stimuli are relevant and equivalent across cultures, and the scoring procedure is capable of measuring the basic variables at issue, a high test-retest reliability coefficient would establish this fact. If the reliability is low, or if it is high in some cultures but not in others, there may be reason to modify the instrument. If the test is not equally meaningful or reliable in all cultures in a study, validity cannot be ascertained. Herein we strongly suggest applying test-retest reliability on projective techniques in cross-national research.

Validity

Nunnally (1967, p. 75) writes "In a very general sense, a measuring instrument is valid if it does what it is intended to do. . . . Validation always requires empirical investigations, the nature of the evidence required depending on the type of validity." Campbell and Fiske (1959, p. 83) note that, in a sense, "reliability and validity can be seen as regions on a continuum. . . . Reliability is the agreement between two efforts to measure the same trait through maximally similar methods. Validity is represented in the agreement between two attempts to measure the same trait through maximally different methods."

Cross-validiation by the convergence of independent methods

We wish to stress the importance of designing cross-national researches so that cross-validation, or convergent validation, techniques may be employed. "Convergent validation" or the "cross-validation by the convergence of independent methods" consists of administering two or more instruments, different in form, which are designed to measure the same variable, and possibly to predict the same criterion. If the variables measured by the instruments are found to be strongly related, in the expected direction, they are held to be cross-validated. At a future date, when cross-national studies are more common and techniques have been developed to assure instrument comparability across cultures, it may be unnecessary to be so cautious and repetitious. But at this stage in the development of research, caution is necessary.

The reliability methods and the cross-validation by the convergence of independent methods technique are designed to establish confidence in the measures of the trait or traits in question. As more languages, cultures, and researchers are involved in a study, the probability of inadequate trait measures is increased. Therefore, the Campbell and Fiske method (or other methods with the same goal) are highly recommended, because they are "primarily concerned with the adequacy of tests as measures of a construct rather than with the adequacy of a construct as determined by the confirmation of theoretically predicted associations with measures of other constructs" (Campbell and Fiske 1959, p. 100).

A construct is measured by a specifically designed instrument. How well that instrument measures the construct indicates its validity. Taking two instruments designed to measure the same construct and comparing the scores from both instruments, we can determine whether they measure the same thing. If they are highly related we claim that they have measured the construct in question and that we have established construct validity.

Campbell and Fiske's point is crucial to cross-national studies. Construct validity is, in a basic sense, tested by this convergent validation technique. In selecting an existing instrument for use in a new culture or constructing a new instrument, researchers must establish content validity when possible, or at least satisfy themselves (and their readers) of its "face validity . . . the extent to which an instrument 'looks like' it measures what it is intended to measure" (Nunnally 1967, p. 99) in the cultures being investigated. The point is that by using reliability and validity techniques, the researcher must establish the adequacy of his measuring instruments. In any research he should do this, but in cross-national research he must; and construct validity, utilizing convergent validation, currently seems the most practical way.

He must have solid reasons for trusting his constructs and instruments because in many cross-national studies predictive validity will not be established. It seems probable that as cross-national research burgeons many researchers will put all their eggs in one "predictive basket." Researchers will try to replicate predictive studies in cultures other than the original. Scientists will want to go beyond the more common descriptive cross-national studies and will look for universal relationships among and between psychological, sociological, and economic variables. There will be disappointments. Expected, predicted relationships will not always be found for reasons inherent in the type and stage of development of research. Predictions may be verified in one or some cultures and not in others. The explanation of these differences in predictive validity cannot be attempted unless previous reliability and validity work has established consistent stable measures of well defined constructs within and between cultures.

Criterion

In cross-national studies in social psychology criteria must be carefully chosen. In cases where the criteria are test scores the precautions for instrument comparability suggested by Nunnally (1967, pp. 76–77) are in order.

> Predictive validity is at issue when the purpose is to use an instrument to estimate some important form of behavior, the latter being referred to as the "criterion.". . . The term "prediction" (is) used in a general sense to refer to functional relations between an instrument and events occurring before, during, and after the instrument is applied. . . . Predictive validity at those three points in time, (has been called) respectively . . . "post-diction," "concurrent validity," and "prediction."

As much care is demanded in securing comparability of criteria as in other variables.

Numerous indices or variables which are not measured in the research but which are extant in the society can be used as criteria. Occupation and school grades are two such variables. Most males in most societies have jobs; many people in different societies will have the same job. But the same jobs in different societies have different social status meanings. In order to use occupational level as a criterion variable across cultures, a scaling system for occupational comparability must be designed.

Grades, the criterion measure of academic achievement in many studies, are vulnerable in any case and particularly so in cross-national research. Lavin (1965, p. 19), discussing comparability of grades as indicators of performance, mentions two uncontrolled sources of variation in grades. First, relating primarily to grade point average, "not all students take the same courses. . . . Second, teachers use different criteria in assigning grades." These sources of variation occur in a single school. But consider the problems of grade comparability across cultures. At age ten, children in some countries will have six years of schooling whereas in other countries they will have had four. Do grades have the same meaning and motivating potential regardless of school experience? Class size may vary across countries from as few as twenty to as many as sixty pupils. Will grades get equal consideration from the teacher when the opportunity and time for contact with pupils must vary with class size? Classes in some places may be composed of students of the same age while classes elsewhere may have an age range of two or three years. Classes may be lecture type in one country and discussion and participation in another. And, seemingly crucial, the education of teachers may range from grammar school and teachers' preparatory school in some countries to specialized teachers' courses and colleges in other countries. Are the same criteria responsible for teachers' judgments in these variant countries? Additionally, grade norms are probably different in schools of different social status levels. In the United States grades or grade point average cannot be considered comparable between, say, high school freshmen at an eastern preparatory school and a rural public high school, or even between middle-class and ghetto schools in the same public school district. Hence comparison of grades is useless unless a school's grades can be corrected for these factors.

This explication does not suggest that grades never be used as criteria in cross-national research. Rather we wish to show that a common criterion variable such as school grades is open to even greater variation in cross-national researches. If in the countries investigated grades are judged comparable, they should be used. But this is a difficult judgment. If they cannot be used, alternatives such as standardized tests may be applicable. In any and all instances comparability of criteria measures is essential.

Social Desirability and Test Validity

The readiness of a person to endorse or agree with a statement on a personality or attitude inventory normally depends on two factors. One is his own personal idiosyncratic attitude or evaluation of the item; the other is his estimation of the social desirability of the item. For example, suppose he is asked which of the following are characteristic of him:

---

1   I do not make new friends easily. _____

2   I like to go for walks with other people. _____

3   I prefer studying alone to studying in a quiet room with other people present. _____

4   I sometimes pick my nose in public. _____

5   I sometimes burp after a good meal._____

It is clear that items 4 and 5 will seldom be checked, while 1, 2, and 3 will get frequent mention. No matter how often he picks his nose or burps after a meal, he will be reluctant to admit it to others because these behaviors are not socially desirable in his culture. Edwards (1957a, p. 85) stated that "the probability of endorsement of a statement in a personality inventory of the Yes—No form or in a Q-sort tends to be positively correlated with the social desirability scale value of the statement."

A teacher is sometimes asked to describe the social adjustment of his pupils by checking the one item of the following pentad which is *most like* a particular pupil and the one item which is *least like* the pupil.

---

a   He sometimes takes the lead in play or work in a small group of friends.

b   He occasionally gets into an argument with a classmate on the school-ground and commences to fight with him.

c He never speaks up in class when the principal or another adult visitor is present.

d He whispers in class about as often as the average pupil.

e He bites his fingernails.

This instrument, known as a *Behavior Description Chart,* identifies pupils who are leaders, aggressively maladjusted, or shy; the teacher's wealth of observation helps to pick out the pupils who are most or least like such statements as those listed above. Statements *a, b,* and *c* are the critical items, but we have added *d* and *e* to serve as *distractors,* or items which do not have any special significance for our study but will allow the teacher to identify the *average* children so that they do not get points for the three adjustment variables we are studying. In this pentad, item *e* will seldom be selected by the teacher because it describes a socially undesirable behavior, and the teacher may not want to make undesirable statements about his pupils. Therefore, item *e* should be replaced by an item which is neutral with respect to leadership, aggressive behavior, and shyness, but equally acceptable or desirable.

Social desirability is defined as a general factor that increases the probability of responding positively or negatively to a question or item of a test, not related to the intrinsic nature of the test instrument. The social-desirability factor must be considered in any study, cross-cultural or not, in which personality inventories or attitude scales are employed. But in a cross-cultural study the social-desirability factor is especially important because of the large variability of the social-desirability factor among different cultural groups. Thus, burping after a meal, or picking one's teeth after a meal, may be considered as a neutral or even a desirable behavior in one culture and very undesirable in another culture.

The researcher should be alert to the problem created by differential social desirability of an item among different cultural groups. Edwards (1957a, p. 8) says: "What is considered socially desirable or undesirable in the way of personality traits is culturally determined. Social desirability scale values of personality statements may, therefore, vary from culture to culture or from judging group to judging group, if the various groups are representative of different populations. We might find, in other words, different scale values for the same set of statements when the statements are judged by males or females, or by different socioeconomic groups, or by different age groups." It would be useful to determine the social desirability of the items of an instrument for the various cultural groups involved, possibly by the scaling methods described by Edwards (1957b), Green (1954), and Guilford (1954).

When an item has variable social desirability in different countries, its endorsement as a self-description cannot be interpreted with confidence as related to cultural differences in a social-pschological variable such as *initiative*, or *autonomy*, or *friendliness*, unless its position on the social-desirability scale is known for each sample. When the differences between countries registered on an instrument are closely related to social desirability of the items determined in these countries, the conclusion had better be that one is mainly concerned with social-desirability differences. But when the differences between countries are independent of the SD scales in these countries, the conclusion that the countries actually differ in the social-psychological variables being studied is justified.

Part Two

Instruments for Use in
Cross-National Research

Chapter 2

Objective Self-Report Instruments

THIS CHAPTER CONTAINS DESCRIPTIONS and discussions of a number of instruments in which the respondent expresses his attitude toward some object or state of affairs. The respondent reports his own personal point of view, though the context may arouse little ego-involvement. *The Uses Test* represents the least ego-involvement, while the Allport-Vernon-Lindzey and the Cattell 16PF instruments most closely achieve a self-conscious involvement of the ego.

Attitude Instruments

Modernity Scales

"Most nations today are development-minded." So Harbison and Myers (1964, pp. 1–2) begin their exciting analysis of the relation between education, manpower, and economic growth from the perspective of human resource development. "The sociologists and political scientists tend to think of development as the process of modernization, and they concentrate their attention primarily on the transformation of social and political institutions. Economists tend to equate modernization and development with economic growth."

"Modern" and "traditional" societies differ on a number of indices. Dr. Ernesto Luis de Oliveira, Jr., a Brazilian social scientist, defines six conditions necessary for a "technological revolution," which exist to different degrees along the scale of countries ranging from "traditional" to "modern":

1   A long and continuous technological experience.

2   Demographic pressure, due to growth of population.

3   Wealth combined with change in the economy; i.e., the economy must be wealthy enough to serve as a base for systematic research and planning, but at the same time must be open to technological change.

4   Social mobility in a social structure that is fluid enough to permit upward mobility.

5   A technical ideology; i.e., an interest in invention and in getting work done in a labor-saving manner.

6   Acceptance of the idea that the state should use its power for the social welfare.

(Havighurst and Moreira 1965, pp. 79–80)

Some of these conditions depend on wealth and past economic history. Some hinge on the prevailing values and attitudes. Social psychologists interested in social change are properly interested in the feelings, the attitudes and values of individuals and groups relative to modernization.

Modernism-traditionalism scales have been developed and employed by social psychologists to measure values (Kahl 1968) and attitudes (Smith and Inkeles 1966) in cross-national studies for over a decade. Kahl (1962, 1968) developed an extensive Modernism Scale for use in Brazil and later in Mexico. The Brazilian scale was abridged by Havighurst and Gouveia (1969) and adapted for a study of Brazilian secondary school students; later Manaster (1969b) used the same adaptation in a study of Puerto Rican adolescents. The OM (Overall Modernity) scales developed by Smith and Inkeles (1966) include items taken directly or adapted from numerous instruments including Kahl's. These two modernity scales were constructed differently and will be discussed separately as prominent examples of modernity scales in cross-national research.

Kahl (1968) analyzed the social science literature dealing with "traditional" and "modern" society and developed a list of characteristics of traditional and modern societies. He then focused on the value or personal perspective aspects of these characteristics. Using earlier research findings and information gathered in conversations with Brazilians, Kahl categorized values about work and career and scaled them as separate variables or dimensions, from the traditional pole to the modern pole. Each hypothesized variable scale, or value scale, included a number of items with which a respondent could agree or disagree. "The first stage of statistical analysis of the answers produced a "series of fourteen scales, each of which measured a basic value that had been hypothesized beforehand" (Kahl 1968, p. 43). The scales were "purified" (low correlating items removed) by factor analysis and the surviving scale items were included in a questionnaire. Some examples of items for specific variables are:

Activism (opposite: Fatalism)
   Making plans only brings unhappiness, because the plans are hard to fulfill. (agreement: traditional faltalist; disagreement: modern activist)

Low stratification of life chances (stratification versus social mobility)
   A person needs good connections to get ahead in the occupational world. (agreement: traditional [ascribed status]; disagreement: modern [achieved status])

Occupational primacy
   The most important qualities of a real man are determination and driving ambition. (agreement: modern; disagreement: traditional)

Low integration with relatives (interdependence on, versus independence from, relatives)
   When looking for a job, a person ought to find a position in a place located near his parents, even if that means losing a good opportunity elsewhere. (agreement: traditional; disagreement: modern)

Seven dimensions—1) Activism, 2) Low Integration with Relatives, 3) Preference for Urban Life, 4) Individualism, 5) Low Community Stratification, 6) Mass Media Participation, 7) Low Stratification of Life Chances—constituted the "core" of modernism. They "are closely interrelated; on the average, a man who is high on some will also be high on the others, although there is room for variation" (Kahl 1968, pp. 21, 42).

A principal-axis factor analysis of Modernism I (the fourteen scales) in Mexico and Brazil showed that the eight items with the highest loadings were the same in both countries, and these eight items were called Modernism II. "The correlation between Modernism I and Modernism II was .83 in Brazil and .84 in Mexico, figures indicating that they are alternative measures of the same dimension."

Havighurst and Gouveia (1969, pp. 279–80) factor analyzed data they collected from Brazilian students using an abridged version of an early Kahl scale. In view of the dissimilarity in samples, the results "are as nearly comparable to those of Kahl as could be expected." Their three factors were described (phrased in the traditional terms) as: "1. Everyone for himself in a world which does not reward real merit and enterprise; 2. Urban society is cold and unfriendly; 3. Live for the present; conform to the mores; count on your family for help."

Kahl (1968, p. 51) concludes: "Whether we use the complex index of Modernism I, or the simpler Modernism II, the pattern is the same: a modern-value perspective is strongly associated with social-status level, and weakly associated with metropolitan-versus-provincial location. Comparisons of groups from Brazil, Mexico, and the United States show no nationality differences when education and urban residency are controlled. Within all three countries the pattern of scores by status level is similar. The regularity of the cross-national results gives additional weight to the reliability of the instrument."

Kahl, like others who have worked with his scales, was disturbed that the vast majority of items were phrased so that agreement indicates a "traditional" response. Since persons of low socioeconomic status tend to be traditional in their responses and deferent in their relationships with status superiors, the question arises whether and to what extent the traditionalism they express signifies their deferent attitude through agreement with items for social rather than conceptual reasons. Kahl (1968, p. 29) believes that "this 'acquiescence set' inflates somewhat the correlations between traditionalism and low status, and may inflate somewhat the loadings in those scales where all the items are phrased in the same direction." Although only two items are phrased in the opposite direction, Kahl concludes that "although 'acquiescence set' is a disturbing element, it is not sufficient to make the results spurious." His conclusion might seem acceptable, but the high correlation between Modernism I and Modernism II (in which agreement with every item indicates "traditionalism") could lead to the opposite conclusion. "Acquiescence set," then, is a factor potentially limiting the usefulness of these scales. Further analysis is suggested on this issue prior to further use of the scales.

The method and process used to develop an instrument is an important indication of the value of the instrument. The two modernity scales we are using for illustration here were, in a general sense, derived by similar methods. Kahl used a form of item analysis to derive his scales, and, in an indirect way, validated them using as his criteria: socioeconomic status, rural-urban residence, and education. Smith and Inkeles systematically used both item analysis and criterion group methods and derived O M measures with each method and a short O M scale consisting of items meeting requirements of both. The similarity of findings suggests that both groups of researchers succeeded in measuring an attitudinal complex which is comparable cross-nationally. However, the procedures Smith and Inkeles used to derive their scales are so compelling that one is inclined to lay greater faith in their final scales.

Smith and Inkeles took items directly or adapted them from a number of different studies including Kahl's, and created many others until they had 119 questionnaire-interview items which covered the thirty-three relevant "major themes" they explored in defining psychosocial modernity. The items were mostly of the fixed-alternative type but there were also a number of open-ended questions. The items were classified as Purely Attitudinal or Behavior-Information items by Smith and Inkeles.

Some examples of items corresponding to specific themes are:

A. Purely Attitudinal Items
   Political Activism
      Have you ever gotten so highly concerned (involved) regarding some public issue (such as . . .) that you really wanted to do something about it?
      1. Frequently   2. Few times   3. Never

General Efficacy

Which is most important for the future of (this country)?

1. The hard work of the people.
2. Good planning on the part of the government.
3. God's help.
4. Good luck.

Openness to New Experience—People

If you were to meet a person who lives in another country a long way off (thousands of kilometers away), could you understand his way of thinking?

1. Yes   2. No.

B. Behavior–Information Item

Mass Media Valuation

How often do you (usually) get news and information from newspapers?

1. Everyday   3. Occasionally
2. Few times a week 4. Never

The interview, including items measuring attitudes, information, and behavior, was administered to over 5,500 men in six countries: Argentina, Chile, India, Israel, Nigeria, and Pakistan. With these data the O M short forms were derived using the item analysis method ("Using the OM Long Form score based on all items as a standard, we ask what sub-set from the larger pool has the strongest relation to the overall score" [p. 362]) and the criterion group method. ("This involves selecting items from the larger pool of 119 attitudinal modernity items on the basis of their power in differentiating known criterion groups" [p. 367].)

Smith and Inkeles set out "to devise a theoretically broad, empirically tight, administratively simple measure of individual modernity which has been widely tested cross-nationally and can be used with little or no adaptation under all field conditions in either research of practical work which requires one to judge the modernity of individuals or groups in developing countries" (p. 376). They would seem to have met their goals satisfactorily. Both groups of researchers found comparable psychological and sociological cross-national relationships. Smith and Inkeles suggest that further research with these concepts can "throw some light on the psychic unity of mankind" (p. 377). Kahl believes that these scales can provide greater knowledge of differences among socioeconomic groups across nations. With either objective, these scales, and scales of this sort which cover broadly attitudinal complexes related to major cross-national theoretical issues, clearly are useful research tools.

Risk-Taking Scale

The Risk-Taking Scale, like the Traditionalism–Modernism Scale, purports to measure a single attitude composed of a number of sub-attitudes or factors. Risk-Taking investigations primarily take two forms: paper-and-pencil attitudinal scale studies, and experimental social psychological studies such as the work of Kogan and Wallach (1964).

Williams (1962) developed a Job Preference Inventory Measure or Risk-Taking Scale as a measure of propensity to take risks as opposed to seeking security, among members of an industrial population. "Through use of Guttman Analysis," he found, "that eight items measuring individual propensity to assume risk belonged to a single universe. . . . A brief examination of the uses of this scale indicated that it has been used to predict level of achievement in the organization, successful and less successful change managers, the attraction of various incentives in the organization and perceived mobility" (p. 8). An example of the eight forced-choice pairs composing the scale is:

Which do you prefer?
A job where I am almost certain of my ability to perform well.
A job where I am usually pressed to the limit of my abilities.

Whyte (1962) has broken the scale into three "facets of entrepreneurial attitude to work. The facets touched upon are: (a) attitude to risk-taking for the sake of success; (b) attitude to work autonomy; and (c) attitude to work which offers challenge as one of its rewards."

Williams analyzed the scale data on personnel in a light and power company in the midwestern United States and concluded that the eight items belonged to a single universe. Whyte, using the scale with Peruvian adults and secondary school boys, and Havighurst and Gouveia (1969), using the scale with Brazilian students, did not find that the items "scaled" in a single universe. Havighurst and Gouveia factor analyzed the scale and found it to be composed of three factors: autonomy, risk-taking, and preference for general rather than specific instructions.

In any objective-type instrument, some respondents do not attempt one or more of the items. Williams included non-responses as nonrisk endorsements. Havighurst and Gouveia gave a modal score for items where respondents did not respond to one item, but excluded respondents who missed two or more items. There is therefore a difference in the makeup of the samples finally analyzed. Havighurst and Gouveia found great variability between Brazilian States in the number of subjects who did not respond to items—3.2 percent nonrespondents to 11.4 percent nonrespondents in the states of Ceará and Pernambuco. This difference in method complicates comparisons.

The Brazilian data provided a basis for comparison of urban-rural, employed-unemployed, male-female, and middle-class–working-class students. Urban, male, middle-class, and employed students scored higher on risk-taking than their comparison groups. Whyte interpreted his findings to indicate that the risk-taking scale depends partly on the attitude of the respondent toward gambling or "taking chances" as well as upon his attitude toward work.

Manaster (1969b) used the risk-taking instrument with Puerto Rican adolescents and found boys to score higher than girls, and middle-class students to score higher than working-class students. Also, the Puerto Rican scores were lower than the Brazilian scores, as a rule.

Because of the question of nonresponses mentioned above, plus difficulties in sampling and linguistic comparability, a truly valid cross-national comparison of these data has not been made. Manaster (p. 10) concludes: "An item-by-item analysis and a comparative linguistic analysis to determine stimulus equivalence across cultures would be necessary before a cross-national comparison is justified, and the ages of subjects would have to be comparable." The cross-national experience with a variety of instruments highlights the frequency of measures of interesting and important variables which have been only partially and unsystematically developed and studied, as in the case of the Risk-Taking Scale. This Scale which represents the attitudes of people toward their work may be of importance in studying the factors related to socio-economic development of a country.

Authoritarianism—The F Scale

Since the publication of Adorno's *The Authoriatarian Personality* in 1950, strong support and equally strong opposition has been voiced about the theory, methods, and conclusions of the study. The study was exceedingly complex, comprised of numerous subsamples tested in various proportions on somewhat comparable batteries of questionnaire, objective-type instruments, and open-ended interview-type instruments. (See Chapter II: Cross validation by the convergence of independent methods.) The literature emanating from this study is large and varied, and not altogether relevant for our purposes. Rather, our discussion of instruments in cross-national research is best served by focusing on one instrument—the F Scale—which illustrates many of the issues raised by the study and which has in itself been used in subsequent cross-national research.

Adorno *et al.* (1950) referred to the F Scale as The Implicit Antidemocratic Trends or Potentiality for Fascism Scale. It has since been called the Authoritarianism Scale (Christie 1954). The initial scale was composed of thirty-eight items which were divided into nine subcategories. The subcategories did not prove to be independent, and the scale can be considered to treat one general factor (Melvin 1955). The items have been said to be vague and ambiguous (Peabody 1966). Some examples of items follow:

Obedience and respect for authority are the most important virtues children should learn.

Science has its place, but there are many important things that can never possibly be understood by the human mind.

Wars and social troubles may some day be ended by

an earthquake or flood that will destroy the whole
world.

Most people are born with an urge to jump from high
places.

When a person has a problem or worry, it is best for
him not to think about it, but to keep busy with
more cheerful things.

Sex crimes, such as rape and attacks on children, de-
serve more than mere imprisonment; such crim-
inals ought to be publicly whipped, or worse.

The items were presented as Likert-type items. That is, responses could be marked from strong agreement to strong disagreement, in this case with no neutral position provided. All
of the items are written so that agreement with them signifies
agreement with an authoritarian statement. The issue of response set or acquiescence set was thus raised. Considerable
work has gone into researching this issue with the F Scale
(Cohn 1953; Bass 1955; Messick and Jackson 1957; and Couch
and Keniston 1960). Brown's (1965) analysis of this issue led
him to conclude, "that a tendency to acquiescence has been a
factor in standard F Scale scores but not the major factor"
(p. 514). The F Scale appears to be an independent valid
measure of the general construct it purports to measure, but
the acquiescence set interpreted as a function of individual
personalities remains a significant factor.

How is this issue relevant to cross-national work with this
instrument? Having established that response sets function
with this instrument in the United States, we must assume
that they function in the same proportion in other cultures if
we intend to compare cultures with this instrument without
additional analysis comparing acquiescence sets.

As we expect countries to differ in compliance or in passivity
we might also expect that they would differ in the proportion
of respondents who need to agree or disagree with items on
written tests. If this is true, then cross-national differences
found on the F Scale might be the result of differences in the
tendency to respond according to response sets between the
countries. This problem with this instrument must be dealt
with. Christie, Couch, and Keniston have attempted to solve the
problem by developing an instrument which balances the items

so that approximately equal numbers of items are phrased as authoritarian and nonauthoritarian assertions. However, the difficulty of developing items that are reversed, in some sense the opposite of the original, is indicative of the cross-national problem of translating such complex items into other languages.

Peabody (1961) doubts that one can translate the items of the F scale from English into other languages. But the Scale has been translated and employed with adequate results (Melikian 1959; Coladarci 1959; Meade and Whittaker 1967). Translation alone appears possible, although the translation of balanced scales has not, to our knowledge, been attempted.

Meade and Whittaker's recent study compared the F scale scores of college subjects in six cultures. Mean scores on the F Scale for the North American sample were significantly lower than all other groups, with Brazilians significantly lower than all other groups except the Americans. The Arabians and Chinese were similar at a next higher level of authoritarianism, and the Rhodesians and Indian samples were the highest in authoritarianism. The interesting fact for this discussion is that the tests were administered in the language used for instruction in the various colleges. Thus English was the language used for the Americans, Arabs, Chinese, and Africans; Hindi for the Indians; and Portuguese for the Brazilians. The spread in mean scores among those using the English language and the fact that the translated instruments produced a wide spread in means leads to the conclusion that the differences are cross-national (if they are not differences in acquiescence sets by culture).

The question arises rather persistently whether the F Scale is a measure of a personality variable describing people with political persuasions solely to the right of the political spectrum or whether it is a measure of antidemocratic attitudes and thus describes persons from the left as well as the right extremes of the spectrum (Coulter 1953; Christie 1956; Eysenck 1954; and Rokeach 1960). Although fascism seems to be correctly the measured variable, as originally stated by Adorno *et al.*, the question would seem to be more fully answered in cross-national research which has the advantage of condoned and condemned attitudes in large sample numbers.

A number of possible problems demanding special care in

translation and interpretation, and changes to eliminate or analysis to assess response set accompany the use of the F Scale. However, the cross-national arena seems particularly suited for study with this instrument. And the prejudices and ideologies which prompted the original studies in the late 1940s are as much with us today as they were then.

Semantic Differential

The study of attitudes—tendencies to accept or reject certain persons, groups of people, ways of thinking, ways of behaving, etc.—is important to cross-cultural research because it provides a brief, quick way to study differences of behavior between various social groups.

Many attitude researchers simply ask people how they feel about things, or what they would do in certain situations, as the most direct way of measuring attitudes. This method, however, does not always predict what the person *actually does*. The person may not really know what he will do in a specific situation, where there are a variety of social forces and of personal considerations pushing him toward a variety of actions. Or, a person may not wish to tell others or even himself what he will do in an emotion-laden situation. Therefore a variety of methods have been devised for the study of attitudes, ranging from the observation of people's behavior when they are making choices, to direct and simple questions about their attitudes, to highly indirect ways of stimulating them to express their attitudes unconsciously.

A semidirect approach has been developed in recent years, using the Semantic Differential. This instrument is something like a game, and most respondents play this game with less inhibition than they would use if they were asked directly to state their attitudes about certain things and certain people. Developed by Osgood *et al.* (1957), the Semantic Differential requires the respondent to place an object toward which he has an attitude on a six- or seven-point scale formed by a pair of opposite adjectives, ranging, for example, from *very good* to *very bad*. Each respondent rates an object such as *My Mother* on each of a number of dimensions, such as strong-weak, happy-sad, hard-soft, etc.

The directions for the test as adapted by Havighurst *et al.* (1965) follow.

We want to know how you feel about various people and things. Beneath the name of each concept or thing you will find a series of scales of opposite words. Locate the person or thing where you think it belongs on each scale.

For example, suppose you have the person, Cowboy, and beneath it the scale Good-Bad.

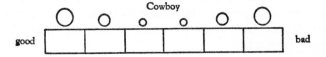

If you think a Cowboy is *very good,* mark a cross (X) in the box under the large circle on the left. Or, if you think a Cowboy is *fairly good* (but not very good) make a cross in the space under the middle-sized circle. But, if you think a Cowboy is only *somewhat good* or *neither good nor bad,* mark a cross in the space under the small circle. If you think a Cowboy is somewhat bad, fairly or quite bad, or very bad, mark a cross in the proper space on the other side of the scale.

Work as fast as possible; do *not* stop to review or think about your marks. We are interested in your first impressions and your real feelings.

This method has several advantages for cross-cultural research. It bypasses the difficulty caused by the fact that people of different cultures may vary in their readiness to express their attitudes on certain matters. The people of one culture may be more "outspoken" than those of another culture. Or there may be certain subjects that are taboo in one culture and not in another. For example, some people may speak more openly about attitudes toward sexual behavior, or toward people of other races.

This method is easy for people who do not read well or are not accustomed to thinking in the abstract way required of a person expressing his attitude on an instrument that asks: "like very much," or "like to some degree," or "am very much opposed," or "am somewhat opposed." The respondent to the

Semantic Differential quickly feels that he is expressing his attitude by marking a point along a continuum, or by marking a big circle as opposed to a small circle. Even fairly young children grasp this concept, whereas they might have difficulty distinguishing degrees of attitude which are defined by words.

The term "semantic differential" comes from the discovery by Osgood *et al.* (1957) that words of different appearance may have quite similar *meanings* and that the common adjectives tend to cluster together into groups when their meanings to people are studied by factor analysis. Most of the common adjectives applied to persons and objects fall into one of three families:

1. Evaluative: good-bad, just-unjust, valuable-worthless, etc.

2. Potency: weak-strong, hard-soft, etc.

3. Activity: active-passive, hot-cold, etc.

The three families emerge as clusters or factors in a factor analysis.

Two questions block the satisfactory cross-cultural use of the semantic differential. First, do the words used to define the adjective scales have the same connotation in the various languages? Researchers who know the nuances of the languages in question may satisfactorily answer this question. A factor analysis of SD scales would give further empirical evidence of the connotations of the words used. Second, do the same factors appear in the meanings of adjective pairs (in the semantic space) in the various languages? Among the European languages this seems to be true, but is it true of Japanese, Chinese, Hindi, etc.? Similarly can adjectives be translated accurately into the languages of indigenous tribal societies in Africa, Asia, and America?

Cross-Cultural Studies with the Semantic Differential. A number of cross-cultural studies have undertaken to discover whether the same factors appear when the semantic differential (SD) is used in different languages (Osgood 1960, 1962, 1964). Jakobovits (1966) applied fifty bipolar scales in fifteen different languages to adolescent males. The languages were:

American, Arabic, Cantonese, Dutch, Finnish, Flemish, French, Greek, Hindi, Italian, Japanese, Kannada, Serbo-Croatian, Spanish, Swedish. The adjective scales were developed indigenously. That is, no attempts to translate adjectives from English into the other languages were made. The fifty adjective pairs were intended to cover the array of meanings in the fifty English pairs. These scales were applied to 100 basic concepts (the same for all languages). The resulting data were subjected to one giant factor analysis. EPA (Evaluation, Potency, Activity) emerged as the first three factors, except for Hindi and Arabic, where rotation of the factor axes also gave an EPA structure.

This study was a severe test of the generality of these factors. Jakobovits (1966, p. 26) concluded: "The fact that each pan-cultural factor is defined by scale loadings of comparable size across all languages proves the true pan-cultural nature of the semantic space as measured by these procedures." Heise (1969, p. 421) sums up his consideration of the cross-cultural studies of the SD as follows: "There is probably no social psychological principle that has received such resounding cross-group and cross-cultural verification as the EPA structure of Semantic Differential ratings."

These studies do not take account of the practical problem of translation of a particular bipolar adjective scale from one language to another. Since the SD is mainly concerned with the connotation rather than the denotation of words, a simple denotative translation may not produce connotative equivalence.

Havighurst (1965) encountered this error in his use of the SD with adolescents in Buenos Aires and Chicago. He started with the following English scales: good-bad, strong-weak, active-passive, hard-soft, just-unjust, happy-unhappy, and hot-cold. Commencing the study in Buenos Aires, he asked a group of mature Argentine university students to translate these scales for denotative equivalence. This did not offer much difficulty, since the English words were common and had fairly obvious denotative equivalents in Spanish. The Spanish version was: bueno-malo, fuerte-debil, activo-pasivo, duro-blando, justo-injusto, alegre-triste, and calido-frio. The only translation which provoked an argument was the hot-cold pair. The first translation suggested by Havighurst to the Argentine students was *caliente*, but they thought *calido* was more fitting. The ordinary Spanish-English dictionaries give these words as synonyms, and give both words as translations of both *hot* and *warm*. They also give the words *caluroso* and *ardiente*, also as synonyms with both *warm* and *hot*.

Havighurst accepted the students' recommendation for *calido*. He computed correlation coefficients for the various pairs of scales as they were applied by Buenos Aires adolescents to a number of concepts, such as Myself, My Father, Girls, Boys, Teachers, Argentina, the United States. He found that the three scales *good*, *just*, and *happy* had high intercorrelation, indicating they fell together into an evaluative cluster, or factor. But he also found that the *calido-frio* scale correlated at about 0.5 with *bueno-malo* and *justo-injusto*, but only .3 with *activo-pasivo*. Thus *calido-frio* belonged in the evaluative factor more than in the activity factor.

More inquiry about the connotations of *calido* and *caliente* indicated that *calido* is closer to the connotation of *warm* in English, and *caliente* is closer to *hot*. But Osgood *et al.* (1967) had used the scale hot-cold, rather than warm-cold, in their studies. Two other researchers have informed us that *warm-cold* has a higher loading on the evaluative factor than on the activity factor when used with Americans, and this agrees with our common American distinction between *warm* and *hot* when these words are used as qualities of people. Osgood's (1957) students used *hot-cold* in a study of Korean and Japanese students in the United States and found that it was highly evaluative for Korean students but not for Japanese or American students. Thus it appears that the words *hot* and *warm* should be translated with attention to their connotative equivalence in studies that use two or more languages.

Construct Validity of the Semantic Differential as a Measure of Self-Esteem. In order to study self-esteem a definition of the "self" is useful. The "phenomenal self" may be defined as a conscious awareness of who one is and how one stands in relation to his environment. This is different from the psychoanalytic concept of the "ego" as a nonphenomenal subjective construct which stands for a configuration of ongoing processes in the personality among which is the cognitive–perceptual function. The "phenomenal self" is an organized configuration of perceptions of characteristics and abilities.

A number of attempts to measure the self-concept have been made with various instruments, such as a Q-sort, an adjective checklist, a personality inventory, and a semantic differential. However, few studies use more than one measure of the self-concept, and therefore the researcher is left with measures from one instrument which has face validity but may also be measuring other things as well as the self-concept.

The "construct validity" of a measure of self-esteem may be checked by comparing its results with those of another instrument which purports to measure self-esteem. If the results of the two instruments correlate to a high degree, they both measure the same theoretical construct, or they have high "construct validity."

Dreyer (1970) attempted to measure the construct validity of the semantic differential for *Myself* used with American Indian adolescents, by comparing scores on a semantic differential instrument with those on a Self-Esteem Inventory. The latter was a set of twenty statements about which the respondent indicated that they were "like me" or "not like me." There were statements such as: "I am a very good student;" "My family does not expect me to amount to much;" "I have many good friends." In order to establish the construct validity of the two instruments it was first necessary to estimate the reliability of the two measures. Their correlation with each other would of course be reduced by any unreliability in either of them. Split-half reliability coefficients of these two instruments when used with Indian adolescents were about .5 to .6. Therefore the observed correlation between the two instruments should be corrected for "attenuation," in this case a considerable correction since the reliability coefficients are low.

In this study, the correlation coefficients of the two instruments used with Indian youth were about .4, uncorrected for attenuation. The correction for attenuation raised the coefficient to .6. Thus, although the two instruments used to measure the "phenomenal self" correlate to a significant degree, they do not have a high degree of construct validity. They both seem to measure some aspect of the "self," but neither can be said to measure the "self" as a whole entity.

Criterion Validity of the Semantic Differential. Little attempt has been made to study the validity of the semantic differential as an attitude measure against a criterion which is undoubtedly valid. Since the "phenomenal self" has been defined as a construct, it is difficult to think of a valid criterion which would measure self-esteem with complete certainty. The "phenomenal self" is defined as conscious awareness of one's characteristics and capacities. How can one measure this without asking the respondent to report on himself? And if he tries to make what he believes to be a socially-desirable response—that is, if he lies about his "self"—who can tell?

Heise (1969) comments that the social-desirability problem appears in the semantic differential, especially for salient concepts, such as "myself," or "my home," or "my native culture." In the example we have given, the self-esteem inventory would seem to be quite transparent and therefore subject to defensive misrepresentation—perhaps more so than the more impersonal semantic differential.

We are inclined to favor the semantic differential for cross-cultural attitude studies because it has been thoroughly investigated, and the pitfalls in its use have been adequately described. However, it is certainly subject to some social-desirability effect.

Social Attitudes (Needs) Inventory

On the face of it, the Social Attitudes or Needs Inventory is an objective questionnaire of people's descriptions of themselves and what they would like to be like. However, additional interpretive approaches with the Social Attitudes Inventory give it a "Needs" analysis function.

The instrument designed by Lucas and Horrocks (1960) consists of a set of statements about hypothetical adolescents and asks the respondent whether he is like the hypothetical boy or girl and whether he wants to be like this person. A sample item might be:

	Yes	No
John has many friends. Am I like him?	( )	( )
Do I want to be like him?	( )	( )

A similar form for girls substitutes a girl's name for the boy's.

The idea of "need" is derived from the pattern of response to the two questions of an item. A subject could respond to the two questions ("Am I like him? Do I want to be like him?") in four ways: *Yes–Yes, No–No, Yes–No, No–Yes*. A response of *No* to the question "Am I like him? and *Yes* to the question "Do I want to be like him?" implies a need, a discrepancy between what he is (perception of self) and what he would like to be (ideal self).

Lucas and Horrocks (1960) originally included 100 statements thought to represent twelve hypothetical categories of psychological needs from a number of behavioral settings. They factor analyzed the *No–Yes* responses from an American adolescent sample and found five factors of need:

I General recognition and acceptance

II Heterosexual affection and attention

III Independence and dominance with respect to adults

IV Conformity to adult expectations

V Achievement in school.

Havighurst *et al.* (1965) adapted the Lucas instrument, selecting the ten items most heavily loaded on each of the five factors, to produce a fifty-item instrument. *The Coping Style and Achievement Study* (Manaster 1970) prepared a forty-item instrument with items developed specifically for the study to describe preferred and actual coping styles in five behavior areas.

The instrument is administered in a group and takes about twenty minutes. Difficulties resulting in the rejection of 7 percent of the protocols in the Havighurst study were also encountered in the Coping Style study. Consequently, the instructions given in administering the instrument should include a full description and demonstration of the four alternative patterns of response to the two questions per item. In this way the great preponderance of *Yes–Yes* and *No–No* responses is lessened and the number of *No–Yes* responses is increased. Nonetheless the large number of *Yes–Yes* and *No–No* responses points to a problem which Havighurst *et al.* (1965, p. 50) describe: "Comparisons of the two national groups shows that the Chicago youth have a greater tendency to express a felt need in all areas than the Buenos Aires youth do. This may indicate a cultural difference not so much in areas of need as in willingness to admit a discrepancy between the perceived and the ideal self."

The data collected on this instrument present a problem of reliability which may in fact appear on other similar instruments. Statements in the instrument may represent situations about which the respondents are ambivalent and to which therefore they cannot consistently respond over a period of time. Respondents may find themselves unable to act (respond) on items too broad for them to comprehend. To guard against these possibilities test constructors make the statements so clear that there can be no doubt about the attitude or situation presented. These statements make for highly reliable items because almost every one either agrees or disagrees with them.

We should expect consistent responses when attitudes are clear and firmly fixed, and we should expect inconsistency when attitude statements arouse ambivalence or when the respondent either cannot understand or does not care and answers randomly. In the quest for reliability of the items and thus of the instrument we may, according to this thinking, find great unanimity of response among homogeneous samples. Whether the variance within these samples correlates with other personality or behavioral variables is yet undetermined. But this type of item and instrument can allow reliable group differences between subcultures: e.g., members of a high SES group may almost unanimously agree whereas members of a low SES group may almost unanimously disagree to particular items; or among cultures: e.g., almost all children in one culture may agree or disagree while in another culture they may give diverse responses because they are ambivalent to certain items or find them too difficult to understand.

Havighurst *et al.* (1965) met the problem of translating the Social Attitudes Inventory from English to Spanish by following the principle of "denotative equivalence." Items which were phrased in adolescent slang or jargon with phrases such as "goes with," "date," and "girl friend," were appropriate enough for American youth but not so for Buenos Aires boys and girls. The translation was done by mature students who were educated in the problems of translation and familiar with adolescent slang. They discussed the translation among themselves and with the senior author when they were unsure. "In these examples: Susie goes with a boy who likes and admires her. Lucy and her date go to the same places and do the same things as other couples do. Dave has a girl friend who seems to understand him. "They translated 'go with' literally as 'andar con,' 'date' as 'cita,' and 'girl friend' as 'amiga.' There was a good deal of discussion about the translation of 'date,' because the practice of dating is different in Argentina than in the United States. Boys and girls do not go out on dates so young in Argentina, and the institution of dating is not so highly developed as in the United States. Furthermore, the term 'cita' has a somewhat guilty meaning, such as 'assignation.' But these are cultural differences, which we are studying" (pp. 43–44).

The argument that without exact translation we cannot compare different national groups seems reasonable. However, it is because of these elusive differences that we must make the comparisons. Our twofold task has been met in the above example. First we attempt to make our translations as comparable as possible in meaning to the subjects, and second we recognize where we might have fallen short and acknowledge this in our reporting and inferences.

In summary, the Social Attitudes Inventory has been used to investigate conscious needs of adolescents and as a self-report of preferred and actual coping styles. The test is easily administered but respondents must be aware of the full range of response options open to them. A real question of the individual reliability of the instrument exists although it can be reliable when used to obtain group data. Once again this is an instrument that shows promise but additional work should be done to assure reliability and validity in future applications.

Values and Interests

For almost forty years "Study of Values: A Scale for Measuring the Dominant Interests in Personality" has been a useful research and clinical instrument. The instrument purports to measure the degree to which an individual personality values six basic types of interest: theoretical, economic, aesthetic, social, political, and religious. This concept emanates from the work of Edward Spranger who assumed that the values a man holds best describe his personality and that all men have personalities describable within these types. We do not acknowledge this last point unequivocally, citing particularly the neglect of "sensuous" values (Allport, Vernon, and Lindzey 1960).

For college students or adults with some college education, the test is easily administered in multiple choice form. For clinical purposes it can be scored by the subject, but supervised interpretation is necessary. For research purposes it is simple to score and gives summed scores for the six values which can be used to make individual profiles. Although "Study of Values" has been used in many different types of researches, it has not been used extensively in cross-national research.

The study of Nobechi and Kimura (1957) illustrates the usefulness and difficulties of the values scale in investigating differences among and within countries. They compared data from students at Japanese Universities with the American college norms in the instrument manual, finding explainable differences between the cultures on religious, aesthetic, and social values. They also found high correspondence between value preferences and the specialized academic fields of the Japanese subjects.

The editor's comment on Nobechi and Kimura's (1957, p. 122) paper points out that

> we must pay attention to the fact that the religious behavior of Christian people is quite different from that of Buddhistic people, and in order to examine the religious attitude of the Japanese people we must put different questions from those of Allport, which is left to our further research.

This point is crucial. Using the same questions as the original instrument, merely translated into Japanese, one finds great differences between U.S. and Japanese subjects' religious values. If the statements and situations for the religious value were truly appropriate for Japan, would one find these same differences? If found would they be the result of responses to truly comparable items?

The problem with using the "Study of Values" cross-nationally is clearly the problem of translating items to maintain connotative equivalence. For many of the items this seems quite possible; however, for others it is not. There would seem to be no problem in translating items of a type which present general statements of an abstract nature, such as: Do you agree or disagree that research should be pure rather than applied? However, there would seem to be a number of problems in cross-nationally translating an item like: "Who do you think is a more important historical character? (a) Socrates (b) Abraham Lincoln." Are the subjects in the colleges in other countries as familiar with these figures as American students are? To what extent would subjects in the U. S. respond to Lincoln chauvinistically? Should Lincoln be replaced in translation with a local-country leader, and if so, is a comparable personage available? Can people, recognizably significant in the development and history of Western Civilization, be thought to have the same image and importance for students from the East, say India or Japan?

Lastly there are items which refer to institutions such as the U. S. Supreme Court, or items such as Leonardo da Vinci's picture, "The Last Supper." These are very well known in the U. S. and have meanings and implications which it would be very difficult to match in other cultures. The question is not whether political institutions or art objects as well known exist in other cultures but whether their value for the population is equally dictated in importance or type. If not, their equivalence as stimuli is highly suspect.

"Study of Values" is undoubtedly a valuable clinical and research instrument in the U. S. It would appear that an analogous instrument can be equally useful within other countries, but the number and magnitude of questions relative to establishing linguistic and stimulus equivalence for items between cultures raises serious doubt about its usefulness for cross-national comparison.

The Uses Test

People growing up and living in two contrasting cultures will show different or contrasting *values* or *cultural orientations*. For example, the United States is a pragmatic and instrumental society, while India's society is spiritual, other-worldly, and idealistic. If this characterization is true, children reared in the two societies might be expected to have different values or orientations. Is it possible to test children and youth for such differences? The test of "Uses of Common Objects" was designed for this purpose.

When children are asked about the uses of common objects, their answers vary from society to society. The functions assigned to objects by the children of a social group indicate the activities, interests, and values that prevail in that group. For example, if children in one society mention boys and girls, stones and water, and money and gardens as functioning chiefly in play, while the children of another society mention these objects more often in connection with work, the one society probably values play while the other society values work, at least for children.

Dennis (1957b) developed the Uses Test to explore this idea. This test contains fifty items of the following type:

                What is the mouth for?_____

                What are hands for?_____

                What is a dog for?_____

                What is a tree for?_____

                What are plants for?_____

                What is a rich man for?_____

                What is sunset for?_____

                What is prayer for?_____

Dennis experimented with lists of common objects, experiences, and actions until he secured a list to which children ten- to twelve-years-old responded easily and with a diversity of answers. For instance, he found that the quesion: "What are the eyes for?" almost always produced the answer: "To see with," and consequently he discarded this item. Eventually a list of fifty objects, actions, and persons was compiled, the referents being universally known and experienced by children. The referents consisted of common objects, such as stones and cats; familiar types of persons, such as boy, grandfather, mother; common human actions, such as shouting, singing, and kneeling; and common experiences such as holidays, travel, and sunset.

Dennis's form of the test has not been published, but a similar list of common objects and actions and persons could be produced by any researcher. Havighurst *et al.* (1965) employed the test in a comparative study of thirteen- and sixteen-year-olds in Buenos Aires and Chicago. The following instructions accompanied the test:

> Here is a questionnaire which asks about the uses of different things we all know. Please write the first thing that comes to your mind when you think of what a particular thing is used for. There are no right or wrong answers and everything you write will be kept confidential. No teachers will see your paper and when we get the papers at the University, we will work from the number on the paper and not your name.

The test took about fifteen minutes. Each item was scored once, although some pupils wrote more than one response to certain items. In this case, only the first response was scored. Occasionally a compound statement was the answer, such as "A Mother is to have children and love them." Here the entire statement was analyzed and the response was said to be *benevolent*, even though the first part, "have children" would have been *instrumental* had it been alone. The responses are scored in the following categories:

Instrumental A life sustaining use, an emotionally neutral action, or a functional use. Examples of the former are "Water is for drinking;" "A tree is to provide food;" while examples of the neutral, functional use are "A knife is to cut;" "Paper is to write on;" "A mother is to bear children."

Benevolent Helping others, receiving help, referring to love, loyalty, friendship. Examples are: "A mother is to love children;" "A lion is to run free."

Malevolent Expressing negative feelings on the part of the respondent or others, ill will, injury, or threat. Examples are: "Hands are for fighting;" "A young man is for war;" "Stars are to make things difficult for astronomers;" "A lion is to growl;" "An old man is to sit around and do nothing."

Hedonistic Reference to objects or actions as sources of pleasure or means of doing what one likes. For example: "Birds are to cheer you up;" "Rain is for playing in puddles;" "A boy is for having dates with girls;" "An old man is to rest;" "Stars are to gaze at."

Esthetic   Reference to beauty in itself, rather than for sensual enjoyment, which would be hedonistic. Examples are: "A garden is for flowers;" "A strong man is to show a perfect body;" "Sunset is for beautiful colors;" "Stars are to adorn the night."

Religious   Reference to deity or to religious practices or to places associated with the supernatural. For example: "The mouth is for prayer;" "A storm is to show God's power;" "Kneeling is to worship God."

Status   Giving or maintaining a position in a hierarchy. For example: "A Queen is to rule;" "A father is for respect;" "A boy is to become a man;" "A grandfather is the head of a household;" "A lion is the king of the jungle."

Intellectual *   The production or nurture of things of the mind. Examples are: "School is for education;" "Paper is to write a book with;" "The mouth is for expressing ideas;" "Silence is to help us study."

Reliability of Scoring

A reader or judge must categorize the responses, and this raises a question about reliability of the scoring. For example, the response "Stars are to wish on" may be benevolent or hedonistic or malevolent, depending on the nature of the wish, which is not expressed. This is a difficult item, but the problem is solved by asking what *effect* the proposed use would have. From this point of view the reference is probably hedonistic, since most people who wish on a star tend to want for some benefit themselves. The responses on "What is *silence* for?" may be categorized as follows: "Silence is for thinking" is in-

* When we discussed the categories with Dennis in 1961, we found that he was developing his procedures for categorization beyond his published work. Our categories differ from those used before 1961 by Dennis in that we added one (Intellectual) and expanded the content of one. Our *Instrumental* is somewhat broader than Dennis' *Sustentative* which refers to uses which sustain life. All but two or three percent of the responses were scorable under our system.

strumental. "Silence is to allow the heart to speak" is benevolent. "Silence is for repose" is hedonistic, and "Silence is to listen" is instrumental.

Problems of Translation

Translating this test from one language to another presents no particular problem since the items represent objects, events, and actions which are universal. The principle of denotative equivalence is followed in the translation.

To score the responses the scorer must be familiar with the prevailing language usages among the respondents. For example, the following responses were given by Buenos Aires youth.

What is a sunset for? La puesta de sol es para contemplar.

What is a mother for? La madre contempla a sus hijos.

What is a boy for? Saber como defenderse.

These would be translated by the unwary North American: "A sunset is to comtemplate" (intellectual); "A mother is to contemplate her sons" (instrumental); "A boy is to know how to defend himself" (malevolent). However, a judge from Buenos Aires would classify the first in the esthetic category and the second in the benevolent category. The word *contemplar*, though translated as contemplate, carries a connotation of deep feeling which in the first case would be wonder and appreciation of the beauty of the sunset, and in the second case would be love and solicitude for her sons. The third response has a familiar meaning in Argentina of preparing oneself for a successful career and would be scored as status-achieving.

For Cross-National Study this instrument may have substantial use as a semiprojective test. It allows the respondent to give what are for him the "natural" responses, without any suggestion that he or his society will be judged by these responses. Clearly, no answers are right or wrong. However, the primary difficulty is defining the most useful categories for scoring the test, and training the judges to categorize the responses consistently.

Rokeach Value Survey

The Rokeach Value Survey has never been used in cross-national research. However, as a recent value-measuring instrument the survey seems worthwhile to consider and analyze for its applicability. The instrument consists of two lists of eighteen values each. One list is composed of "instrumental" values, which refer to modes of conduct such as courage, responsibility, honesty, etc., and the other refers to "terminal" values, which refer to end states of existence such as beliefs in salvation, equality, world peace, etc. All of the values are socially desirable and subjects are required to rank-order the values according to their importance to them.

Rokeach ran reliability and stability studies on a sample of Michigan State University students (Hollen 1967). He found reasonable reliability with this sample; median reliability for the terminal values was .78 to .80 and for the instrumental values it was .70 and .72. He found

> that various combinations of these terminal and instrumental values significantly differentiate men from women, hippies from nonhippies, hawks from doves, policemen from unemployed Negroes, good students from poor students, fifth-graders from seventh-, ninth-, and eleventh-graders, retail merchants from sales clerks, Jews from Catholics, Democrats from Republicans, and so forth (Rokeach 1968–1969, p. 555).

Value differences were also found between churchgoing and nonchurchgoing college students, those who participate in civil rights demonstrations and those who are unsympathetic to the cause (Rokeach 1968–1969), and among a variety of political positions (Rokeach 1969). The value survey appears quite useful for determining value patterns of Americans of college age or older. What then are the indicators of this instrument's potential usefulness cross-nationally?

The values included in the lists and the manner in which they were selected provide a beginning. Wanting only positively evaluated, socially-desirable values, Rokeach reviewed the literature, interviewed students and adults, and utilized the Anderson (1968) and Allport and Odbert (1936) personality trait lists. He distilled these tests to include independent, culture-broad values that individuals would admit to "without appearing to be immodest or boastful" (Rokeach 1969, p. 6), considering a full range of values which should have cross-national significance.

However, before using the instrument in other countries, we should determine the degree to which the values included in these lists cover the prominent values recognized for the countries being investigated. If these values cover the broad spectrum of important values in a country the instrument would be effective. However, significant values might be ignored. If these lists are incomplete a cross-national study employing the Value Survey could still be a valuable comparative study of the values in the survey. However, one would be unable to characterize a society or group by these values alone if there were indications that other prominent values were not included. The value survey therefore seems to be applicable but should not be used blindly; the values within the countries being studied that are known or thought to be important must be looked at in relation to the values of the Survey.

There is a real question about the effectiveness of this Survey with subjects under college age, and no published data provide the answer. The brevity and level of abstraction of the value statements may necessitate some minimum level of education of subjects. This, of course, is speculation, but a number of the values would seem difficult for people with less than high school education to evaluate. This might be particularly problematical in a cross-national study in which, for example, middle-class adults in two countries differ significantly in their educational backgrounds.

The section on Stimulus Equivalence in this book covers many issues which pertain to the difficult translation of this instrument. When a translation includes many modifying words it is considerably easier to achieve equivalent meanings than when a translation consists of one, two, or several words. The Value Survey consists of one or two word "names" of the values and one to five words amplifying or explaining the "names." With precise work, suitable translations are possible; one must be cautious, however, in using an instrument cross-nationally which heavily depends on few abstract words.

The Rokeach Value Survey is potentially useful in cross-national research. We have tried to point out some of the obvious pitfalls. The purpose of this section was to illustrate an approach to choosing an instrument which has no cross-national history but which may be used in the future.

The Occupational Values Questionnaire

The usual method of studying the values of children and young adolescents is to ask them what kind of work they would like to do—or what kind of job they would like to have. Instead of asking them for their preferences among occupations, one can describe various kinds of work in terms of the values people may seek or gain, and ask for their preferences among these values.

One such instrument was used in the Cross National Study of Coping Behavior (Peck *et al.* 1970). It presents fifteen possible reasons for desiring a certain kind of work. The reasons are categorized as follows: Altruism; Esthetics; Independence; Management; Success and Accomplishment; Self Satisfaction; Intellectual Stimulation; Creativity; Security; Prestige; Economic Returns; Pleasant Surroundings; Desirable Associates; Variety; Follow Father's Occupation. The subjects were directed:

On the pages which follow, you will find 110 pairs of statements. Each pair has two statements which talk about different kinds of work. You should read each of the two statements carefully, and then circle the letter (a) or (b), in front of the statement to show which of the two kinds of work you would rather do.

Here are some examples:

    a   Work in which you could lead other people
    b   Work in which you can one day become famous.

Another one is:

    a   Work in which you can help other people
    b   Work in which you can be with people you like.

The instrument repeats the pairs in all possible combinations of a pair of values. Thus the respondent states a preference between each value statement and all other value statements.

The fifteen value-categories were chosen from the literature on occupational values. The statements were deliberately simplified, so that they could be read and understood by children as young as age ten. Five of the pairs of statements were repeated in the Questionnaire, so that the consistency of the responses could be determined. If answers were purely random, the percentage of agreements between two identical pairs would be 50, and the percentage of agreement on all five pairs would be 3.1. On the other hand, if the answers were repeated with complete consistency, 100 percent of the responses would be in agreement. In fact, the percentages of complete agreement varied from 3 to about 30 among various age and nationality samples in the study, with the Japanese and Mexican groups showing less consistency than other groups. However, all the groups responded with consistency more than half of the time, the percentage of consistent responses on at least three of the five pairs ranging from 75 to 92.

As noted in Chapter 2, some inconsistency enters when the respondent is ambivalent, and therefore answers one way at one time, and another way at another time. An advantage of this instrument is that the social desirability factor is about the same for all items. They are all stated in socially acceptable terms. Another advantage is that only a few crucial *words* must be translated with complete connotative equivalence. The sentence as a whole conveys the meaning and can be easily translated into a similar sentence in other languages.

The validity of the instrument as a measure of values has not been tested against any outside criterion. The items do have face validity. By being attached to the concept of an occupation or a type of work, they are made rather impersonal for children and young adolescents who are not yet thinking seriously about their own occupations.

The chief preferences of fourteen-year-old boys from six countries, in order: Self Satisfaction, Success, Security, Intellectual Stimulation, Creativity, Pleasant Associates, Altruism. The least preferred was Esthetics. Age differences and nationality differences account for more of the variance than do sex and social class.

This instrument promises to yield useful comparative data. Whether it is a good measure of values is another question.

Probably a cross-validation with one or more other instruments that purport to measure values would be useful.

Personality Inventories

The California Psychological Inventory

One of the more widely used personality inventories is Gough's California Psychological Inventory. Gough worked at the University of Minnesota on the Minnesota Multiphasic Personality Inventory and acquired a substantial background of experience with personality testing before he put together the self-report inventory known as the CPI. Consisting of 480 items which are marked "agree" or "disagree" by the respondent, the Inventory gives eighteen different scores. The items that make up the subscales were selected if they were answered differently by a criterion group than by the average respondent. The criterion group consisted of young people who were rated by people who knew them as having certain personality characteristics, or who showed other more direct evidence of having those personality characteristics.

The Inventory can be administered as a total instrument, or its subscales may be selectively used. Gough and his students have used a number of the subscales such as the Socialization Scale with respondents of various nationalities, to test their validity cross-culturally. Otherwise known as the Delinquency Scale, this segment of the inventory attempts to distinguish between impulsive, delinquency-prone persons and persons who are well "socialized"—i.e., who adequately control their impulses and understand and respect social stability.

This scale was translated into Spanish and used with adults in Costa Rica and Puerto Rico. Gough (1965) felt that he had established its validity in these two countries. Translations were made into the Spanish to achieve denotative equivalence. Connotative equivalence was not a problem since the items did not refer explicitly to law breaking, law observance, or societal stability. However, some items required special attention to the problem of connotative equivalence. One of these was the English item: *Lincoln was a greater man than Washington.* Since few Latin Americans would be sufficiently familiar with the characteristics of Lincoln and Washington to make the kind of judgment expected, Gough modified this item to: *Juarez was a greater man than Bolivar*. This seemed to achieve connotative equivalence for Latin Americans from Mexico and Central America. Juarez and Lincoln were rather alike in personality and in political role, as were Bolivar and Washington.

Havighurst used this inventory with sixteen-year-old students in Buenos Aires. Knowing that neither Juarez nor Bolivar was well known to Argentines, Havighurst asked a group of university students with whom he was working to revise this item with persons known to residents of the Argentine. They came up with the item: *Sarmiento was a greater man than San Martin*. San Martin, a soldier, was "the father of the country" to several South American republics. Sarmiento was a liberal leader during the latter part of the nineteenth century. He was ambassador to the United States from Argentina during a part of Lincoln's presidency, and they became good friends.

In fact the mean scores on the Socialization Scale were very similar for Buenos Aires, Costa Rican, and California youths, which may be evidence that the instrument is valid for cross-cultural research if certain items are carefully adapted. Gough and his students and colleagues have investigated the cross-cultural validity of certain scales of the CPI (1960, 1964, 1965, 1968) with what they regard as reasonably positive results. The scale has been translated into German, French, Spanish, Japanese, and Hindi.

The validity of certain scales of the CPI has been investigated by comparing the scores of contrasting groups, who do and who do not show unmistakable signs of the behavior predicted by the scales. For example, juvenile delinquents have been compared with nondelinquent youth on the Socialization or Delinquency scale. The scales prove to have a degree of validity when tested this way, but the two contrasting groups overlap in scores somewhat, and therefore the CPI cannot be used to describe the behavior of specific individuals, even though it may be used to describe the average behavior of a group of persons.

The Cattell 16 Personality Factor Questionnaire

A short section dealing with the work of Raymond B. Cattell can hardly do justice to his voluminous output. However his systematic approach to personality testing, accounting for cultural similarities and differences, should not be ignored. For more than two decades Cattell has been building and refining the theory and research associated with his 16 Personality Factor (16 PF) Questionnaire. For background reference the reader is directed to his *Personality and Motivation Structure and Measurement* (1957), and the *Handbooks* (1959–63) produced at the Institute of Personality and Ability Testing.

The Institute describes the 16 PF as

> a factor analytically developed personality questionnaire, designed to measure the major dimensions of human personality comprehensively, in young adults and adults from sixteen or seventeen years to late maturity.*

The test purportedly measures two levels of personality dimensions. The first, the *primary* dimension level, is composed of sixteen factors, such as Factor A which is described as Reserved to Outgoing, Factor L—Trusting to Suspicious, Factor O—Placid to Apprehensive. The second level is composed of four composite "second-order" scores derived from combining the primary factors. The Institute says that:

> they are rougher, and lose some information, (but) they nevertheless provide an even more convenient capsule-description of personality, frequently in meaningful categories closer to everyday parlance.

The four principal second-order 16 PF composites are: Anxiety, Extraversion-*vs*.-Introversion, Tough Poise-*vs*.-Responsive Emotionality, and Independence-*vs*.-Dependence.

We will not attempt to deal in depth with the 16 Personality Factor Questionnaire (16PF) as any summary investigation of worth would necessitate far more space than we have available. Rather this section will point to the work with the 16PF as a good example of detailed, quantitative, systematic instrument and theory building which takes into account the needs and requirements of cross-national research.

Cattell has directly addressed himself to some of the questions that interest us. He says:

---

* Institute for Personality and Ability Testing (Champaign, Illinois), descriptions quoted here are taken from advertising material for the 16 PF.

The first systematic studies on the cross-cultural constancy or change of personality factors were those of Cattell, Pichot, and Rennes on the French-English comparison of the 16 PF and of Cattell and Warburton on the British-American comparison of personality structure in children's questionnaire responses. Comparisons have since been made on the 16 PF in Italy, in Germany, and in Japan.

In all of these cross-cultural comparisons, in terms of the personality sphere, the clear verdict so far has been that, at the primary-factor level, a very high degree of similarity of personality structure exists among these countries and cultures. . . . The primary finding is one of essential similarity or constancy of basic personality structure. The secondary finding is that, despite the foregoing, there are interesting and apparently significant differences of expression (factor loadings) on certain variables and significant differences on the factor level.

No justification would exist for comparing populations on common scales unless prior research had shown that the same general primary factors exist in the personality structure of both groups. . . .

Although marked progress has been made toward cross-cultural comparisons at the primary-source-trait level [i.e., traits such as: intelligence, ego strength, dominance, surgency, superego, etc.], very little knowledge indeed has been gained at the secondary-source-trait level (Tsujioka and Cattell 1965, pp. 207–209).

Cattell states that attaining meaningful cross-cultural population measurement and relating and comparing these measurements in the study of group behavior and personality is crucial. Although there is ample justification for using the primary source traits across cultures, the task is not always practical, and studies utilizing the secondary-source traits might be more advantageous. However, the cross-cultural stability of the secondary source traits is not confirmed. "Entering upon the construction, translation, and use of such scales becomes worthwhile, however, only when there has been investigation of the comparability of second-stratum source-trait structure across a number of cultures" (Tsujioka and Cattell 1965, pp. 207–209).

Cattell presents us with both the primary and secondary traits which cover a very broad spectrum within the area of personality research. Cross-national research with the primary traits is flourishing (Liu and Meredith 1966; Butt and Signori 1966). More cross-national research utilizing the second-order traits is in progress (Meredith 1966) but, as Cattell stresses, more is needed. The rationale for the detailed research that has been carried out is clear. The methodological considerations, especially the statistical issues, have been worked out and spelled out with utmost care. For researchers interested in the areas Cattell has investigated and the approach he has used, the 16PF and more specific instruments for investigating second stratum traits such as the IPAT Anxiety Scale (Scheier and Cattell 1963) are highly recommended.

Chapter 3

Projective Instruments

THIS CHAPTER ANALYZES five projective instruments which have been used in many cross-national studies investigating personality factors, attitudes, and values in comparative group perspective. Each instrument instructs the subject to respond in a particular form, verbal description, completion, drawing, to general stimuli such as story or sentence stems, pictures, or instructions. The individualistic responses are relatively unstructured and considered to be projections of the individuals' personality.

Sentence Completion

The Sentence Completion Test contains "stems" or incomplete sentences which the respondent makes into complete sentences. The stem may be short, such as: "I like . . . . ," or well structured, as: "The worst thing a teacher can do is . . . ."

This has the appearance of a projective test; it might be called "semiprojective." Experts in projective testing support the general statement that a sentence completion test reveals attitudes and values at the conscious level. Thus, Henry (1960, p. 628) writes, "In general, this instrument is seen as providing information on attitudes, motives, and conflicts at a more conscious level rather than on the structure and organization of personality."

In his discussion of the sentence completion test as a means of predicting overt behavior, Bertram R. Forer differentiates between "extrinsic prediction," when a test predicts overt behavior in certain situations, and "intrinsic prediction," when a test predicts a pattern of attitudes, motives, conflicts, defenses, etc., which are not necessarily overt. For a given person "the data vary with the stimuli, often appearing contradictory. Contradictory responses are taken to represent different levels of psychological functioning and organization." Accurate prediction requires complete assessment of all the inclinations and controlling mechanisms and all the situational possibilities as well. Extrinsic prediction is more likely to be successful the more structured and unambiguous the test situation. "The manifestation of a trait, wish, activity, or affect in one test or at one psychological level carries with it little or no indication that it will occur at another psychological level or in a particular situation" (Forer 1960, pp. 6–17).

This skeptical view is not shared by Duijker and Frijda (1960, p. 78) who discuss the use of projective tests in cross-national studies. They say:

> The Sentence Completion Technique has not yet been used very often in cross-cultural research. Its value here and in other fields of character and personality studies may all the same be regarded as proved. It appears to tap attitudes and values of a high level of personal involvement, and to permit inferences as to personality trends. Comparison of results is not too difficult, both as regards intranational consistencies and cross-national divergencies.

The consensus is that a Sentence Completion Test should agree with other tests of attitudes and values, expecially if it contains stems in the first person, such as "When they put pressure on me, I . . . . ," which elicit a more direct report of a subject's reaction than a stem in the third person, such as "People often expect . . . ."

However, any test is at best only a partial predictor of overt behavior. Generally the Sentence Completion test is positively correlated with results from attitude inventories or questionnaires. For example, using the following item on a Sentence Completion test, what can we infer from the completions?

It is good . . . .
A   to work hard and make money.
B   to obey your parents.

At face value A indicates an autonomous and instrumental value attitude, while B indicates a dependent attitude, that would also be indicated by checking the "agree" column of a personality inventory which contains items of this nature. On the other hand, we might say that responses A and B are "free associations" to the stem, which might arise from a guilty conscience, in the case (A) of a lazy person, or (B) of a disobedient child.

There is also the question of "censorship." Suppose we have the stem: "At times I . . . ," and we analyze the completions for evidences of interest in heterosexual activities. Are we to suppose that the response "think about having a date" is evidence that the subject wants consciously to have the company of the opposite sex and that he would indicate that he agreed with the following statement on a personality inventory: "I want to have dates with girls (boys)." Or are we to suppose that the person would not allow himself to make this response when directly asked about his desire to have dates? Further, are we to suppose that both sexes are equally frank in admitting an interest in the opposite sex? Or will girls be more inhibited than boys from saying they want dates in answer to a direct question, while they will be more likely to give responses on a sentence completion test that indicate an interest in the opposite sex?

The Sentence Completion test is generally used for the study of attitudes or dispositions to act. Usually a number of stems are used which elicit responses belonging in a certain category of action. For example, a certain SC test with fifty stems was used to measure the following dispositions (Havighurst *et al.* 1965): Instrumental vs. Expressive orientation, Autonomy vs. Dependence, and interest in Heterosexual Activity. In order to avoid scoring all fifty items of the Sentence Completion test for these three variables, and because most of the sentence stems were not designed to elicit responses which could be classified in one of the three categories above, a few items were selected for further analysis. Two judges went through a number of protocols, indicating for each of the fifty items whether it stimulated responses which could be classified in one of the three categories. The items that both judges placed in one of the categories a reasonable number of times were retained for analysis in that category. In this fashion ten items were selected for scoring on the Instrumental-Expressive variable, eleven items for the Heterosexual and seven items for the Autonomy-Dependence variables. Some of the items could be scored for more than one variable.

Scoring System and Reliability of Raters

The responses to the ten items measuring the Instrumental-Expressive dimension were rated as Instrumental, Expressive, or Indeterminate. The responses to the items measuring Autonomy-Dependence were similarly rated as Autonomous, Dependent, or Indeterminate. Heterosexual interest was simply scored "present" or "absent."

The 400 items rated by each judge (from forty protocols) on the Instrumental-Expressive variable, showed 72 percent agreement, 19 percent partial disagreement (one place on a three-step scale), and 9 percent flat disagreement (one judge rated a response as Instrumental while the other rated it as Expressive). The Autonomy-Dependence variable, showed 73 percent agreement, 23 percent partial disagreement, and 4 percent flat disagreement. The Heterosexual interest variable showed 96 percent agreement.

Criteria for Rating on the Instrumental-Expressive Variable. Responses to the ten stems selected for analysis were scored as Instrumental when they exhibited: a) a concrete means to achieve a goal; b) a future state that requires instrumental action; c) if they contained an active, instrumental verb; d) if they referred to some instrumental property of an action or state. For example:

I feel proud when. . . .	I finish making something (c).
	I play the trumpet (c, d).
	I get a good grade (b).
My father. . . .	works (c, d).
	wants me to work tomorrow (b).
Some day I. . . .	hope to be a mother (b).
	will join the Air Force (b).

Responses were rated Expressive when they indicated (a) emotion without instrumental connotations, (b) indeterminate future states that contained elements of wish-fulfillment. For example:

I feel proud when. . . .	I'm successful (b).
	they talk well of me (a).
My father. . . .	Is a good egg (a).
	Is nuts (a).
Some day I. . . .	will be rich (b).
	will be famous (b).
	will die (a).

Responses which did not fit either category were scored as Indeterminate. In particular: responses that limited themselves to a definition of the stem, or that contained a passive verb without implying emotion, were so classified. For example:

I feel proud when. . . .	I am acknowledged.
	I eat.
My father. . . .	Is a man; is thoughtful.
Some day I. . . .	will be 6 feet tall.
	will be like Peter.

The Sentence Completion Test in the Study of Groups

Although the SC test can be interpreted by a clinician who does not need to compare the responses of two people, this test is more often used by social psychologists in the search for group differences. Groups can be compared for differences related to age, sex, socioeconomic status, ethnic status, etc.

The statistical significance of group differences can be studied in two ways: each test item can be treated as a unit, or each individual can be treated as a unit. When test items are taken as the unit of study, two groups of subjects may be compared on the percentages of their responses in a given category, such as Autonomy. This method indicates the significance of a difference in average test score between the two groups, with a given difference becoming more significant as the number of items increases.

A more stringent test of group differences treats each individual as a unit, and allows him to be counted only once in group comparison. In this case the individual is placed in one or another category on a given test. That is, for the Instrumental-Expressive variable a person is classified as "instrumental" if at least six out of his ten responses are classified as instrumental, "expressive" if at least six responses are expressive, while he is classified as "indeterminate" if less than six responses are classified in either the instrumental or the expressive category.

Need for Achievement

Another method for analyzing the Sentence Completion test is to score the responses for some underlying attitude that is being expressed by the respondent. For example, the responses might be scored for optimism, or pessimism, or hostility. In this case we analyzed the test for the basic need for achievement (nAch) defined by McClelland *et al* (1953) and measured by him with a form of Thematic Apperception Test. Peck has devised a method of scoring the Sentence Completion test for nAch, and we followed his directions. Each item is scored according to whether the sentence as completed contains reference to achievement and whether the reference is positive or negative in tone. Certain stems of the test which generally bring out a stereotyped achievement response are omitted in this scoring procedure. The following examples of Peck's scoring system applied to specific stems show, in order, positive, neutral, and negative responses:

When they put pressure on me. . . .
    . . . I try to stand up to it. (*positive*)
    . . . I eat. (*neutral*)
    . . . I crack. (*negative*)
If I only had. . . .
    . . . better grades in school.
    . . . some money.
    . . . no homework.
When other people do better. . . .
    . . . I try to do better yet.

> . . . I'm glad for them.
> . . . I'm discouraged.
> Secretly I. . . .
> . . . am smart.
> . . . want to be liked.
> . . . don't like school.

When scores on the SC test were compared with scores for the same students on McClelland's TAT test for Need for Achievement, the correlation coefficient for twenty boys was only .07, indicating that the two tests as they were being scored were not measuring the same trait.

Language Problems in Cross-Cultural Comparisons

The SC test used for cross-national comparisons presents two kinds of language problems. The more simple is how to interpret a frequent response in one language, when respondents using another language apparently do not give this response. For example, in the Buenos Aires-Chicago study the stem, "The best thing about my mother. . . ." brought completions from 40 percent of the Buenos Aires youth with the word "bondad," (goodness), while only 2 percent of Chicago youth said "She is nice," or "She has a nice personality," or "She is good." It is difficult to decide here whether there is a real difference between the two groups, or whether the language difference poses an artificial kind of interference.

Translation of the Test. The most severe problem is that of translating the test so that the stimulus value in the two or more languages is the same. Since the sentence is unfinished, the translation problem is more difficult than where a complete sentence is to be translated. If two languages have different grammatical structures, unfinished sentences are especially difficult to translate.

The easiest case is the translation between English and Latin-derivative languages (Spanish, Italian, Portuguese, French) since the word order is substantially the same. The modern versions of these languages have largely abandoned the dative, accusative, and ablative case endings on nouns.

But translation between English and a more inflected and

rule-bound language such as German raises severe problems, due to the inverted word order of the German principal clause when preceded by a subordinate clause, and by the fact that the German has two different forms for dative and accusative, while the English has only one. The English version has a number of stems of the form: "When people ignore me, I . . . ." Here the emphasis is on the *I*, which forces the completion to be the responsibility of the writer. But in the German, the inverted word order requires a verb before the subject, and the stem cannot be translated with the word *Ich* without a preceding verb. Thus, the German translation of the stem above must be:

"Wenn andere Leute mich nicht beachten, dann. . . ."

("When other people do not notice me, then. . . . ")

This must be followed by a verb, and the respondent may respond with an action of himself (then I don't care.), or of other people (then they are unpleasant). Thus, for these ten *I*-stems, the German and the English forms are not truly equivalent. This was solved by limiting the response to an action of the respondent. For example, "When someone hurts my feelings, I. . . ." "Wenn mich jemand beleidigt, dann. . . Ich. . . ." The other problem is that a stem like "My Mother . . . me," can be translated either with *me* in the dative or accusative. We give both alternatives. (a) Meine Mutter. . .*mich*. (b) Meine Mutter. . .*mir*.

Another way to overcome this obstacle was to revise the stem: "Most people . . . .other people." Instead of giving two versions (dative and accusative) of *other people*, this stem was written:

"Anderen Leute gegenueber sind die meisten Menschen. . . ."

("Toward other people, most people are . . . .")

This is clearly not a fully satisfactory version of the English stem.

Problems due to different *word usages* as well as different language structures are illustrated by the stem, "When my parents make me mad, I. . . ." A Spanish translation is "Quando mis padres me hacen enojar, Yo. . . ." But this sometimes called forth, from Mexican children the responses, "I forgive them," or "I have to apologize," or "I repent." Other countries almost never produced this kind of response. Was the difference one of parent-child relations, or was it a difference of language usage?

For a student of languages, we may give the translations used in Italian and Portuguese.

"Quando i miei genitori mi fanno arrabbiare, io . . . ."

"Quando meus pais me frazem ficar com raiva, eu . . . ."

Are these really equivalent?

The Germans have great difficulty with this stem. One translation is "Wenn ich mich ueber meine Eltern aergere, dann. . . ich. . . ." Another is "Wenn mich meine Eltern in Wut bringen, dann. . . ich. . . ." Still another is "Wenn ich geaergert bin durch meine Eltern, dann. . . ich. . . ."

Even more difficult for a westerner to grasp is the problem of translating these stems into Japanese or Chinese. The Japanese have different forms of expression for communicating with people of different statuses. There is a *polite* form, and a more direct form. The child's responses to stems which are meant to stimulate emotional reactions will probably depend somewhat on the form of language which is used in the stems. Depending on the speaker's position with respect to the hearer—sex, age, familiarity, social status—the Japanese pronoun, verb, verb ending, and adjective alter without changing the word order. There are more than twenty ways of saying the word *I*, and each of these has its own peculiar nuance in terms of the speaker's respect, familiarity, or contempt for the listener. Thus the beginning of a stem in Japanese tends to set the tone for the completion, and to limit the respondent. In translating a Sentence Completion stem, the emotional nuance must be preserved. The process of correct translation resembles the process of translating poetry.

Word order in Japanese is different from word order in English. For instance the Japanese verb generally comes after the object, rather than before it as in English. Therefore the notion of a sentence *completion* is different from what it is in English where it generally means adding the last few words of a sentence.

In spite of these differences and difficulties, the Sentence Completion test can be useful in comparing groups from different countries, provided the researchers are wary of the language pitfalls.

Story Completion Methods

Story completion methods have a long history in the field of psychology. Although problems are inherent in the method, and others result from use in cross-national research, there appear to be some advantages to its use. Lansky (1968), in a complete historical review of the use of the story completion method, its assets and liabilities, concludes (p. 319) that the use of story completions have run full cycle starting from

> more or less phenomenologically-oriented studies of complex personality processes by such famous persons as Hartshorne and May and Piaget. Then, a predominantly clinical projective testing orientation held sway with strong emphasis on the task as servant to the clinician's judgment and intuition. Lastly, we have seen a swing back to research interest in story completion methods and new emphasis on structured stimuli—stimuli which pinpoint and control certain variables in order to test specific theoretical hypotheses. Today, the subject matter tends to be specific in that information about particular mechanisms, attitudes, motives, situations, etc., are being sought rather than general descriptions of "whole" persons: defense mechanisms, moral standards, responses to moral situations, complex motives, and the like, not so much from a phenomenological view, however, as from a careful analysis of some particular theory. These new studies have pointed up both the promise and the problems for the future of story completion methods.

The story completion method consists of the presentation of the beginning of a story which the subject must complete. Specific questions delimit areas to be covered in the completion. Constructing a story completion method may look easy; however, issues relating to the story beginning as stimulus, scoring the completions, and projective technique assumptions make the use of this method complex.

The Story Beginning as Stimulus

The beginning or stem is the stimulus in the story completion method. For cross-national research two related issues about the stimulus in projective devices, the degree to which it is structured and the comparability of meaning are pertinent. The relationship between these issues is complex. Less structured stimuli hold little or no cultural meaning or prior personal meaning for subjects and, therefore, could be comparable across cultures. However, the variety of meanings a test of this sort theoretically can have in different cultures, and the enormous range of possible responses to an unstructured stimulus, make difficult the researcher's task of adequately determining the source of the differences he finds. Is the difference because the test is stranger to people in one culture than another, or does imagination have greater importance here than there?

An unstructured stimulus should elicit a broader range of responses across groups and should elicit more information from the individual as he is required to form the story almost from the beginning. The unstructured stimulus fits Frank's (1939, p. 402) stipulation that projective method stimuli be relatively unstructured and free of "cultural patterning" so that "we elicit a projection of the individual personality's private world because he has to organize the field, interpret the material and react affectively to it." Cronbach (1949, p. 433) stresses the value of the unstructured stimulus.

> The projective test uses a stimulus even more unstructured than the situational test—if possible, one so novel that the subject can bring to it no specific knowledge of how to respond. . . . Projective tests come nearer to grasping "the whole person" at once than any other testing technique.

Unstructured stimuli elicit responses which cover a wide range and allow interpretations of the "whole person." However, in cross-national research these advantages may be disguised disadvantages.

Just how wide and varied the range of possible responses to unstructured stimuli could be in a cross-national study is debatable. A model such as all possible personality types subdivided by creativity and verbal ability multiplied by nation, culture, subculture, and family might indicate the scope of responses plausible in this type of research. Imagine then, scoring all of these responses in terms of the "whole person."

At this early stage in cross-national studies research questions are limited by theory, operationalization, and inexperience. We are not ready to deal with and interpret "whole persons" across nations. We have to ask more limited research questions in areas such as defense mechanisms, moral standards, complex motives, etc., which are the types of specific subject matter currently considered by story completion methods.

Examples of vague, unstructured story beginnings translated by Würsten (1960, p. 193) from the Madeleine Thomas stories * are:

---

9 It is evening. The boy is in bed, the day is ended, the light turned off. (a) What does he do before going to sleep? (b) What is he thinking about? (c) One evening he cries, he is sad. What about?

10 Then he goes to sleep. What does he dream about?

11 He wakes up in the middle of the night. He is very much afraid. What of?

An example of a structured story stem from Anderson (1961, p. 484) Incomplete Stories illustrates the presentation of a specific situation representing one problem, conflict, or dilemma.

The teacher suddenly discovers that fifty cents has disappeared from her desk. She looks up and sees that all the class are working on their arithmetic. She wonders what happened to the money and what she should do.

What does the teacher do?

Finish this story also with a few sentences. Tell what happened to the money and also exactly how the teacher feels and what she does.

Assuming that structured stems are more useful, at least at this stage in cross-national research, how does this effect the problem of comparability of stems? It is difficult to devise stems which are comparable regardless of whether we are constructing unstructured or structured stems. The basis for lack of comparability in unstructured stems is as vague as the stem. In structured stems, lack of comparability across nations can be pinpointed. It will emanate from either the situation presented in the stem or the language of the stem.

In the Anderson example the fact of missing money, the class

---

* Not all Madeleine Thomas Stories have vague beginnings. Some have a definite, specific, clear structure. We refer you to the original article by Würsten (1960).

working, and the teacher's internal conflict, seem patently obvious and natural. Researchers from each country can judge whether it seems appropriate for their country. No reason is apparent for lack of comparability across nations. However, two aspects of this story stem may cause difficulty.

First, the sex of the teacher may be inappropriate in some cultures or some schools. Should the sex of the teacher in the stem be uniform regardless of the sex of the teacher in every subsample, or should the sex match? Second, is fifty cents a great deal of money or a trifle? The amount of money missing may be a gauge for some subjects of the magnitude of the problem. Should the amount of money missing be the same regardless of the socioeconomic status of the subjects? Should the money missing be a figure equal to say, the amount it would cost for three lunches for a child? Should the fifty cents figure be converted to the proper national currency according to current international monetary exchange rates?

The participants in a study would have to make decisions about these two potentially troublesome points. Their decision would be dictated to a degree by the countries involved. That is, if all participating countries were highly industrialized Northern European countries, these questions could be more easily resolved than if the participating countries varied greatly in standard of living and type of school system. No matter what decision is made differences in meaning across countries will remain. The decisions will be made with the intent of minimizing these differences. The differences in meaning that remain will have to be accounted for in analyzing, interpreting, and reporting the data.

Scoring Story Completions

The scoring methods for story completions vary from highly intuitive clinical readings to elaborate content coding methods. Certainly cross-national study has no place for intuitive, personal, idiosyncratic scoring procedures; no comparability across scorers across nations would ever be reached. But content coding is particularly appropriate to cross-national studies. Anderson and Anderson (1961) use this method and report (p. 484), "A coding manual for content analysis has been constructed for each story. The categories in the coding manual have been derived and defined from the content of the children's story completion." On the face of it this method is logical and straightforward: the areas of investigation are categorized and analyzed according to the actual productions of the subjects and not fitted into predetermined categories which may or may not coincide with the children's stories, although they fit perfectly the researcher's bias. In most studies a content coding analysis is worthwhile even if the codes are later systematically collapsed according to some theoretical framework. The content coding method is relatively "clear;" the researcher's bias does not dictate the codes; the subject's responses do.

To illustrate a content coding system with the Story Completion we will use examples from the Coping Style and Achievement Study. An analysis of a content coding system developed for this study with Sentence Completion and with Story Completion instruments can be found in a paper by Michelis (1969). However the Story Completion analysis gives a more complete picture of the constructs included in the system and will be discussed here.

Eight stories were presented for completion in the Coping Style Study. The variables in question for each stem were the same for all stories but the nature of the stories were such that the content for each could elicit a variety of classifications of responses. The eight story stems represented: *interpersonal relations, aggression, authority, anxiety,* and *achievement* situations. The stories could therefore vary considerably, but the scoring system was designed to measure the important common variables or dimensions while maintaining the uniqueness of each story through the individual content codes for that story.

The major dimensions of the coding system are representative of the major variables, while the coding categories under each variable represent the content codes specific to each story. Examples of the types of variables under study in this example are: (a) categories for describing in some manner the sequence of action engaged in by the hero with reference to the problem, (b) categories for classifying the initiator of these various types of action, (c) categories for describing whether the problem is solved completely by the hero or with the help of others in some way.

One story stem for an achievement and interpersonal relations situation (Michelis 1969) is:

> Mary's teacher suggested that the class write a paper over the weekend. This was extra work that the teacher did not usually ask them to do. If they did it they could get extra credit toward their grade in class. On Sunday Mary was getting ready to go out with some friends when she remembered the paper. Mary . . . .

The following categories represent the variables listed above, and the codes represent the content breakdown within each category.

I. Mary's intentions or cognitive stance with regard to the two activities.
   A. She intends only to write the paper.
   B. She intends to write the paper first and then socialize.
   C. She intends to socialize first and then write the paper.
   D. She intends to socialize only.
   E. Her only intentions involve some unrelated activity.

II. Nature of the action.
   A. The first action involves a decision-making process as to which activity to pursue.
   B. The first action is that of planning or beginning to write the paper.
   C. The first action is that of letting the friends know she cannot go out with them.
   D. The first action is that of socializing.
   E. The first action is an attempt to write their papers together.
   F. The first action is the pursuit of some unrelated activity.

III. Initiator of the first action.
   A. No mention.
   B. Mary initiates.
   C. One or both parents initiate.
   D. One or more of the peers initiates.
   E. One or more of Mary's siblings initiates.
   F. Some other person initiates.

IV. Degree of implementation by others.
   A. Mary does not ask for or receive any help.
   B. She asks for but does not receive help, so pursues it by herself.
   C. She asks for and receives help.
   D. She receives help which she has not requested.
   E. Someone else pursues the activity for Mary with no participation on her part.

The sequence of action categories (II, III, IV in this example) are repeated for possible second and third actions in the story. In this scheme the data, the actual story completions, account for the type of information coded; the previously determined constructs, however, account for the delineation of major categories.

Problems of Personal Bias. As long as individuals make choices an element of personal bias exists in a system. However the content coding system built, as it is, on the responses of the subjects limits the scope of scorer bias in the system.

Essentially the process of developing a content coding system begins with categorizing a sample of responses according to the similarity in their meaning, i.e., how they fit together. This is presented as an "empirical" approach. In trying this approach one finds that responses will "fit together" to a degree but one should also acknowledge that the way in which they fit together is in part a function of the categorizer's perception of his task. That is to say that two people independently categorizing the same responses may not come to the same classification system. However the content codes will probably be more similar than if they developed their codes *a priori*.

In the second step the content codes are matched with the theoretical constructs under study. This necessitates another injection of coder bias but still rather openly relates the raw data to the system. This process also allows responses to be included in the system which were not anticipated prior to data collection. And, of course, this constitutes a test of whether the story stems elicited responses relevant to the constructs involved.

If a researcher intended to carry out a study in his neighborhood, with his children and their friends, he might assume that he could predict fairly completely the type and range of stories the children would produce. He might be wrong. He would feel less assurance as he moved from his area and culture. In cross-national research we might feel we command sufficient knowledge of our own nation to construct a scoring system without looking at finished stories first. We would probably be wrong. In a cooperative cross-national study researchers from all participating nations could pool their predictions in a scoring system. They not only might be wrong again, but they could conceivably never agree. By using a content coding system they not only let the data determine the coding categories, they also assure that the scoring codes represent the stories of the subjects even if these stories bear little or no resemblance to the researchers anticipations.

The Story Completion as a Projective Instrument

> Among users of story completion tests, the projective hypothesis . . . seems to be accepted. The subject or client is assumed to 'identify with' the hero: male, female, man, beast, third person, first person or whatever. Because of this identification, the individual then unwittingly reveals areas of his or her personality whether or not he is consciously aware of them (Lansky 1968, p. 313).

Grinder and McMichael (1963) in a cross-national comparison used story completions as measures of personal guilt and found no consistent relationship between the projective measures and actual behavior rated for resistance to temptation. Their findings with the story completion are in line with "a problem familiar in projective testing: The responses to the projective test do not correlate consistently with supposedly relevant overt behaviors" (Lansky 1968, pp. 306–307).

This problem will have to be dealt with by research in the future. For the assumption is still operative among users of projectives that areas of personality, personality patterns, dimensions of cognition, motive statements, and attitudes toward self and others, can be measured by projectives, and therefore by story completion methods. Most, if not all, of these elements of the psychology of the individual should be discernible in his behavior; maybe in specific behaviors but certainly in general behavior patterns. It seems equally justifiable here to question the description and rating of behavior as the weak link in the correlation with projective measures as it does to question the projective measures themselves.

With group rather than individual data, which are more common in cross-national studies, the story completion method has proven value in differentiating between nations. Anderson and Anderson (1961) examined the responses of children in relation to some general hypotheses about their cultures and the children's perceptions of the teachers as representative of the cultures. They tested over 9,000 subjects in seven countries. Their study, although it has sampling shortcomings, exemplifies a cross-national hypothesis testing research using the story completion. They labeled nations authoritarian or democratic, and hypothesized that children's endings to the stories would show attitudes and behavior theoretically related to the child's "type" of country. For the most part the data support their hypotheses. They conclude (pp. 491–492):

> Projective techniques are noted for their uncertain reliabilities and validities. Cross-national research which necessarily deals with values and other symbolic systems is beset with difficulties of definition and control. High internal consistency with responses of large numbers of children in different cultural and national locations has been found. It is concluded that the Anderson Incomplete Stories are a projective device which can with some validity be used to differentiate educational values and value systems in interpersonal relating in different cultures.

Lansky notes that the "tension-seeking," "competence," "effectance" (White 1964; Dember 1965), and "new" view of motivation, as well as the new look at "coping" mechanisms as parallels to some defense mechanisms (Kroeber 1964), have not been used in the theoretical development of story completion methods. He is optimistic about these possibilities. As this book is being prepared, the study titled "Coping Styles and Achievement: A Cross-National Study of Children" is in the data analysis stage which includes story completions being rated for "coping style" and "coping effectiveness." The principal investigators from the eight countries involved in this study have high hopes for this use of the story completion.

Manaster (1969a), in an unpublished dissertation, found

high predictive validity for "coping style" and "sense of competence" related to achievement. They were measured from a story completion instrument developed for the Coping Style and Achievement Study. Further research investigating the relationship between coping style, as measured by the story completion, and actual behavior should shed light on the use of this framework and the projective-behavior correlation. Nonetheless the relationship between these concepts and school achievement, which is an evaluation of behavior, bodes well for the validity of the story completion method in future applications of these perspectives.

It seems quite useful, therefore, in cross-national studies, to use story completion methods with well structured story stems and a content coding scoring system for a wide variety of types of investigations. The method allows specificity of research questions, elicits depth of response (a projective characteristic), allows statistical analysis plus personal reading and interpretation of the response, which is not possible with objective methods, and facilitates inclusion of all responses gathered while eliminating the necessity of an *a priori* scoring system with its possible bias.

Thematic Apperception Tests

The Thematic Apperception Test, the TAT, is a popular psychological instrument in the clinical and cross-national research fields. But the actual TAT, the test developed by Morgan and Murray (1935), is only one of many sets of thematic apperception techniques. Murray developed a set of pictures to which subjects told stories, and he presented a system and rationale for scoring these stories. With Murray's personality theory, and an analysis of the needs and presses of the stories, a clinician could theoretically describe personalities. Clinicians have therefore used Murray's TAT pictures extensively, albeit with highly individualistic interpretive styles.

Rosenwald (1968, p. 218) summarizes the TAT:

> The TAT [is] a multipurpose and multidimensional technique whose immense promise is very widely recognized today. Yet the test is still far from completely understood; some of the assumptions made in the clinical use of the TAT do not yet rest on solid scientific ground. And what is even more astonish-

ing is that much which is known on the basis of impeccable experimentation is still of rather indifferent value to the clinician for whose sake it is being ascertained. The clinical utilization of the TAT is making great strides nevertheless, and the knowledge gained about the test through systematic research continues to be of momentous importance for many fields of psychology.

In addition to what we have learned from research *about* the TAT and its benefit to clinicians, research *with* the TAT has also brought important results.

In this section we intend to cover broadly some of the uses of the TAT method and to caution some of its usages. We also want to stress the multiplicity of pictures or cards which have been used under the name of TAT and the variety of analytic techniques that have been employed. As an example of the magnitude of techniques, Neuringer's chapter in Rabin's (1968) book discusses the Children's Apperception Test, the Picture Story Test, the Michigan Pictures Test, the Make-A-Picture Story Test, the Blacky Pictures Test, the Object Relations Test, the Four Picture Test, and the Picture Arrangement Test, among others. All of these tests are distinct from the standard TAT and are referred to by name. A number of versions of the TAT have been developed for particular groups, such as Negroes, American Indians, South African natives, army recruits, and parachutists. Special forms of the TAT have been developed for specific purposes such as measuring motivational states, particular aptitudes, interests, and attitudes.

The number of tests and researches using TAT is testimony to the esteem in which the method is held by psychologists of all persuasions. But the variety of TAT versions also presents a problem. The basis for many forms of the TAT is that the pictures should represent persons and situations typical of the race, culture, and subculture of the respondent. But respondents would not usually become personally involved in test items in a foreign language; similarly, respondents will not "project" themselves into pictorial situations that are "foreign" to them.

When different sets of cards are employed in different countries or subcultures the comparability of the findings is dubious. And yet the pictures *must* be different. The most effective way to minimize this effect is to strive for maximum comparability between similarly intended pictures across cultures using one set of cards as the standard. For example, using the Murray cards as the standard, pictures adapted for other cultures could parallel particular pictures. This set is particularly appropriate because some of the cards do not contain referents specific to any one culture. These cards, used in conjunction with adapted cards in a comparative study, allow a systematic analysis of the effects of the different cards. Duijker and Frijda (1960, p. 77) mention another procedure which would benefit future cross-national researchers:

> We also want to suggest that research using the Murray series should, in its selection of plates, keep in mind other investigations; even if plates did not seem necessary for the immediate research purpose, they might still be administered in order to enable later comparisons.

Researchers could have greatly extended analysis and comparison had they used a standard set of the Murray cards or specific adaptations of them from the beginning of cross-national research with the TAT.

The Standard Approach to Analyzing TAT Stories

Two of the most respected early cross-national TAT studies were undertaken by Caudill (1952) and by Henry (1947). Caudill's study is more appropriate in the context of social-psychological research because it presents more systematic quantitative data. However Henry's study is invaluable for the diligence with which he describes the evolution and final application of his technique. As a discussion of considerations inherent in employment of the TAT in cross-national research and a systematic resolution of many of these problems, Henry's paper is a classic.

Henry set out to investigate whether the TAT, which had been used with acceptable results in the white, American, middle-class culture, would yield equally valid results in other cultures. He used a form of the TAT especially drawn for applicability to Navaho and Hopi Indian subjects and was able to compare his results with data from other instruments on the same subjects, all part of the Indian Education Research Project.

Henry first proved to his own satisfaction that useful information was elicited by his variation of the TAT. Then he carried out a validity study to determine whether the TAT analyses of individuals discriminated clearly between them. Although the amount of experience with and knowledge of the cultures involved influenced the accuracy of matching personality descriptions from the TAT, Rorschach, and life history, all judges correctly matched a significant number of cases. The conclusion, therefore, was that the analyses of individuals by the TAT was specific to the individual.

The second validity study carried out by Henry illustrates the method of "cross-validation by the convergence of independent methods." The TAT was analyzed, according to a scheme Henry developed, in terms of seven major functional areas: mental approach, creativity and imagination, behavioral approach, family dynamics, inner adjustment and defense mechanisms, emotional reactivity, and sexual adjustment. Each of the other instruments in the Indian Education study (Rorschach, life history, a test battery, and a free drawing) was analyzed for statements on the same functional areas as in the TAT. The statements were judged to agree or disagree with the TAT statements for the same individual. The interpretations from the TAT showed a high agreement with the other instruments. From these two validity studies Henry (1947, p. 82) concluded:

> As can be seen in the foregoing quantitative analysis and as was clear from the qualitative analysis in the clinical conference, the TAT had cut across and integrated all the other techniques used in this research . . . the TAT gave personality descriptions that were consistent with other known data on the case and which also contributed new and helpful information on the personality of the subject. The analyses gave a general picture of the personality structure and the emotional development of the individual and, in addition, provided this description in a behavioral and social context that made possible demonstration of personality variables in overt behavior and of the motivational background of behavior.

The final portions of Henry's study contain generalized psychological descriptions of the two Indian groups. These descriptions have been checked by anthropologists and found to be consistent and valid. Nevertheless the quantitative material and statistical comparisons are sketchy. However, Henry was attempting to prove the usefulness of the TAT cross-culturally in this study, and he accomplished this aim. Henry has since developed a scheme for comparing groups with the TAT (Schaw and Henry 1956).

A more recent comparative TAT study by Gutmann (1966) on aging males in the Maya in Yucatan illustrates the use of the instrument in contrasting cultures for hypothesis testing purposes. This study also illustrates the strength of TAT studies or any cross-cultural study that builds on past research in a direct replicatory way. The study is relevant historically because the cards include seven especially drawn for this group, and four from the Henry study and four of the standard Murray cards. Additionally Gutmann's intent was to compare his Mayan findings with those from a U. S. sample he had previously studied (Gutmann 1964). His work exhibits the continuity of research interest and design, both by type of cultural group and subject area, which is missing from much of the TAT and other cross-national research.

Gutmann's (1966) is a hypothesis testing study and careful consideration of cultural sampling is evident. He eloquently explains (pp. 247–248) his rationale for selecting a culture to test his hypothesis.

> A developmental hypothesis of personality change is most stringently tested by comparisons of different cultures whose child-rearing styles, value orientations, economic systems, and age-grading systems are significantly varied. The particular hypothesis considered here—that men age along a continuum delineated by the active, the passive, and the magical styles— was drawn from American data and is best tested in societies where older people are respected, where they have an advisory role toward younger people, and where they tend, with increasing age, to amass political, ceremonial, and magical power less available to the young. In these respects, American society is notably negligent of the aged; and so it is not surprising that older American men show regressive ego changes. However, should the age-graded trends found in American data also appear in materials drawn from older men in societies that assign them honor and power, a theory of extrinsic social influences could not explain the agreement between these cross-cultural findings. The existence of intrinsic developmental factors that pattern and delimit ego functioning

in later life would be logically demonstrated. The above considerations suggested the Yucatan region of Mexico as a site.

The scoring procedures for this study are spelled out in the earlier American study; however, the basics are presented in this article. Henry's position that "each card contains a latent stimulus demand" (Gutmann 1966, p. 248) is the point of departure for the analytic procedure. The latent stimulus demand for each card was determined "through review of all the stories elicited." This aspect of the procedure seems highly dubious and yet is a frequent approach. By taking all stories in the sample and categorizing them according to an "inductive" approach into "natural" groupings seemingly all of the decisions are based on the scorer's theory, bias, and biased perception. The possibility of replicating findings in the same culture or other cultures is greatly reduced for other investigators because of the personal nature of the scoring scheme. A content-coding system such as the one illustrated in the Story Completion section permits the use of a sample of stories for determining individual (culture-specific) codes while maintaining the theoretic construct system for overall analysis.

The efficacy of Gutmann's cards is instructive. The Mexican cards produced for the study elicited stereotypic responses. The stimuli seemed to have the same connotation for all Mexican subjects, and they responded in what appeared to be the socially acceptable manner. The Murray cards and the American Indian cards "elicited fairly idiosyncratic interpretations, data that reveal more clearly the age differences in perception and interpretation" (Gutmann 1966, p. 249). It would seem that cards which are too familiar in content will not, particularly in "passive cultures," elicit individualized responses but rather stereotypic acceptable responses. The subjects respond as they think their peers will. Perhaps we need not go so far as we have in developing new and unique sets of cards for different cultures.

Remembering the questionable nature of the scoring procedure, the quantitative handling of the data by Gutmann (1966) is clear and directly related to his hypothesis and the American data to which he compared it.

Once all the data for a particular card had been analyzed, the response distribution, by thematic subgroup and by respondent age, was tested for statistical significance by the chi-square method (Gutmann 1966, p. 249).

Analyzing each card individually makes the data quite specific and accents the repetition of findings. On the other hand total score type analysis is impossible, therefore quantitative comparisons cannot be made and the conclusions and comparative discussion must be of an inferential nature. As in Gutmann's (1966, pp. 256–257) summary of the similarities of the American-Mayan findings:

> Age-related trends in the form and content of Mayan peasant TAT stories replicate to a large extent age-related trends in the form and content of American TAT stories gathered from an urban sample of similar age and sex composition.

The popularity of the TAT in cross-national research appears to be well founded. The numerous problems that have been discussed should be dealt with in the interest of validity of particular studies and replicability of findings. The time and effort expended in its development seem well spent.

The Specific Purpose Approach to Use of the TAT

Achievement motivation has been measured by a number of methods but the most frequent measure is the TAT. Since McClelland and his associates began their enormous output on the subject (McClelland *et al.* 1953; McClelland 1955; Atkinson 1958; McClelland 1961) others have followed suit. By ingenious analyses from a variety of cultures on such artifacts as literature and art objects, McClelland measured achievement motivation. However, McClelland's method of scoring TAT stories for achievement motivation is the most relevant.

Brown (1965, pp. 473–474), in summarizing "The Achievement Motive," says:

> Since there is no single clear criterion against which to validate a measure of achievement motivation we found that the validation process amounted to a demonstration that scores on the measure related to other kinds of behavior in such a way as to satisfy our intuitive notions of achievement motivation. In the end, however, something more than this has come of the very numerous studies relating Achievement Motive scores to other data. The scores are higher for managers than

for other sorts of professional men; they are related to economic growth; they go with a taste for moderate risks, long range planning, and tasks that involve clear criteria of success and failure. The process of validation has turned into a process of reconceptualization. The measure now seems to be primarily concerned with motivation for economic achievement rather than with achievement motivation in general. . . . The standard pictures may be a little more effective for eliciting achievement imagery in the economic sphere than they are for eliciting such imagery in other spheres.

Brown's statement identifies three issues we will consider: the cross-national validation of the technique, the cross-national efficacy of the picture stimuli, and the implications of the economic emphasis in multinational research.

The method for procuring achievement motive scores involves presentation of four standard pictures (although different pictures have been used and a rating system for choosing pictures exists [Birney 1958]) to which subjects respond with stories which are scored according to a standard content analysis method. A validation type study, experimental in nature, measures achievement imagery in situations which are considered neutral or situations which might arouse the motive. A second type of study measures achievement motivation in relation to demographic characteristics of the subjects or familial, child rearing attitudes and behaviors. The third type compares levels of achievement motivation between groups within and between cultures.

The first type of study considers the question of cross-national validity. Angelini's work is a fine example of the replication of the experimental validation type of study in another country. He concludes that the method is reliable and valid for studying human motivation in Brazil (Angelini 1955, 1966). Angelini measured achievement motive according to McClelland's technique for groups of subjects under neutral, success, and failure conditions and found results validating the assumptions of the technique. Although some assume a technique such as McClelland's, which meets with such success, to be universal, the need for validation studies in other countries remains, not only for the technique itself but for the scoring system.

The work of Rosen (1962, 1964) is the most well known and

highly-regarded cross-national research exemplifying the two usual types of study. Rosen compared American and Brazilian families and found differences in achievement motivation between the boys in the two countries and in the family structure of their homes. He also compared groups in the two countries in relation to economic growth and found differences in the same direction, i.e., the Brazilians lower in achievement motivation.

Rosen used a technique that had been judged reliable and valid for the countries in which he worked. The standard content coding system for achievement motivation is an enormous asset for its cross-national application. The authors questioned Rosen on his use without alteration of the content coding system developed by McClelland in his work in Brazil. In personal correspondence he replied:

> No important changes had to be made. The one change which was made involved very few of the more than 700 people to whom I administered this test in Brazil over the past 10 years, and that has to do with scoring references to specific occupations as evidences of achievement imagery. As you know, McClelland regards imagery about professional occupations as, for example, physicians or lawyers, as evidences of achievement motivation because they involve a notion of long-range planning. Perhaps this is true in the United States, but I do not think it is necessarily so in an underdeveloped country like Brazil where many people are not at all familiar with the training that is necessary to attain professional status. Therefore, I did not score a story about becoming a doctor, or lawyer or poet unless the story involved some reference to excellence of performance. That is to say if the subject fantasized about becoming a "good" lawyer or doctor or what have you, that was scored as achievement imagery, but if there was no reference to quality of performance the imagery was not scored as indicating achievement motivation.

Rosen's rationale is clear; however, deviations from a standard scoring procedure can theoretically account for some portion of the differences between the groups scored in different ways. Rosen has indicated that responses were not consistently scored in both countries. Regardless of how "few" of these responses exist, the statistical differences he found were weighted differently. Assumptions and changes, such as those

Rosen made, if presented in print, assist the reader in properly interpreting the findings and allow other researchers to proceed with like studies more knowledgeably.

The question of emphasis on economic achievement in this research and the associated issue of indices of economic growth are pressing indeed. They have not yet been resolved satisfactorily.

Convergent Validation of Achievement Motivation

Achievement motivation has been measured with a variety of instruments. In some instances cross-validation of the measures has been attempted through use of independent measures with varying degrees of success. The following examples illustrate two different outcomes.

LeVine (1966) studied differences in what purported to be *achievement motivation* between three Nigerian ethnic groups by three methods—analysis of dream reports, written expressions of values, and public opinion survey data. The three sets of data confirmed each other, and led to acceptance of the proposition that the Nigerian groups actually differed on achievement motivation.

On the other hand, Havighurst (1965) studied achievement motivation among Buenos Aires sixteen-year-olds with three methods—a TAT, a Sentence Completion Test, and a Social Attitudes Inventory. The TAT was administered to small groups of sixteen-year-old students by projecting the six slides on a screen, and giving the respondents five minutes to write a story after viewing a slide for thirty seconds. The directions as prepared by McClelland were translated literally into Spanish. The procedure was introduced as a "test of imagination." The request to write stories based on pictures was within the experience of Argentine students. The pictures were all of males, similar to achievement motivation pictures used in the United States. For instance, one picture showed a young man sitting at a book-laden table, with a clock in the background showing the hour to be late. Another picture showed a young man sitting by himself at a table in a student dining room, with a nearby table full of students obviously having a good time. The clothing was such that it was not considered unusual by Argentine respondents. Probably the pictures had the same denotation for subjects in Buenos Aires as for North Americans of the same age. For example, a picture of a young man and an older man standing near a fence against a rural background was generally placed by Argentine respondents on the Argentine pampas without question.

The TAT protocols were scored for Achievement Motivation by four judges (three South Americans and one North American) who had been trained to use a modified version of the McClelland method and who scored the protocols "blind"— without knowing anything else about the respondent, and without knowing his standing in the Sentence Completion or the Social Attitudes instruments. The Sentence Completion test consisted of fifty items, selected from a larger test prepared by Robert F. Peck of the University of Texas. This set of items had been chosen with the aim of scoring the test for achievement motivation. Peck had used a Spanish version in studies in Mexico City. A few of the items were changed slightly to fit the Argentine usage of Spanish. He prepared a scoring manual for positive and negative affect in relation to achievement themes whenever they appeared in the completions given by the respondent. Achievement themes were identified by both explicit and implicit reference to some standard of excellence. Achievement motivation was measured by counting the number of completions that implied a *positive* identification with successful achievement and subtracting from this the number of *negative* completions, which implied identification with failure to achieve. Each of the four judges scored one-fourth of the protocols to avoid a bias toward high or low scoring by a particular judge.

The Social Attitudes Inventory defined one category of items as *Achievement*. The respondent answered the question "Do I want to be like him?" *Yes* or *No*, in the case of such items as: "John always does his very best when he has a task to perform."

For comparison of the three instruments or methods, the protocols of twenty sixteen-year-old boys from Buenos Aires were chosen; the twenty boys having an almost rectangular distribution on the Sentence Completion Test, so as to get a wide range of scores. Rank-order correlation coefficients were computed. For TAT and SC, this coefficient was +.07; for SC and Social Attitude score, the coefficient was +.01; and the correlation between TAT and Social Attitude score was also insignificant.

Thus the method of convergent validation did not support the use of these tests to measure Achievement Motivation among Buenos Aires boys. If one of the methods could be established as valid on other grounds, then the other two would have to be regarded as nonvalid.

Another "Specific Purpose" Application of the TAT

The work of Coelho and his colleagues (1962) illustrates good use of a special set of TAT cards designed for a particular purpose and used cross-nationally. They "were interested in devising an economical and reliable psychological instrument for measuring the coping behavior potential of adolescents during their college freshman year." They developed a set of ten "Student-TAT" pictures which they considered representative of new and problematical situations to entering college freshmen. The simple and reliable rating scheme pinpointed three variables in the problem solving sphere: solution or resolution of the problem situation, activity in bringing about the resolution, and a determination of whether, in light of the story hero's goals, the resolution was favorable.

In the U. S.:

> the test, given to three groups of college freshmen, decisively differentiated between a clinically disturbed group (Ward Group) and two normal groups, state university freshmen, and exceptionally competent freshmen, who had been screened independently for behavioral competence (Field Group). Ss in the Field Group project a view of college culture wherein problem situations are manageable, and the student is coping with these problems through active effort and optimism. The Ward Group by contrast projects a view of college culture in which problem situations yield few, if any, solutions; and the student is characterized by projecting few solutions, relative passivity and pessimism (Coelho 1962, pp. 364–365).

The study was replicated by Field *et al.* (1963) in Puerto Rico using the same TAT cards and scoring procedures and Field reported (p. 198):

> Student-TAT results showed that fantasies of active mastery, directed striving, and optimism were most prominent in a highly competent group of Puerto Rican students selected for

superior academic, social, and extracurricular abilities, and
were least prominent in a group of emotionally disturbed college students.

This work indicates that the use of a projective instrument
like the TAT for measuring a concept like "competence," which
might theoretically be culture bound, is justified. It also shows
the value in creating a set of cards for a specified purpose
when the intention is to replicate the use of these same cards
on other cultures. Lastly the authors of these studies point out
that their cross-national samples may not be as different as if
they had chosen more contrasting culture samples, and their
findings are thereby limited. Also according to Field (1963, pp.
197–198) they do

> not attempt to answer the question as to whether there is
> greater motivation for mastery or competence in the United
> States than there is in Puerto Rico, but rather whether dif-
> ferent student groups within each culture show similar pat-
> terns of fantasy response to key problem situations in
> adolescent development.

This conservative level of analysis is well founded and in keeping with their research objectives. They were investigating the
possibility of a universal strategy for competence in a specific
age group and found it in two cultures. Until and unless this
pattern was found in additional cultures and the scores themselves equated statistically they were not justified in comparing
the cultures as higher or lower on their variables. They satisfactorily met their objectives, in a particular area with a TAT
instrument developed for their purposes, without overstepping
the bounds of cautious interpretation.

The Rorschach Test

The Rorschach Ink-Blot test is an objectively scored projective
test that has been extensively used to diagnose personality. Its
period of greatest popularity was between 1930 and 1960. Since
the test can be scored objectively, with relatively little training, it is generally used by anthropologists and psychologists
for cross-cultural studies; they feel more sure of themselves
with an objectively-scored test than with one requiring clinical
judgment.

The test measures qualities of thinking and the nature of

ego-mechanisms involved in the control of impulse or affect. It enables clinicians to make inferences about the mental health of the respondent. George De Vos (1966, in a working paper), anthropologist and psychologist, has said:

> There is considerable controversy today, among those who have concerned themselves with the study of mental health trans-culturally, whether one can presume validity for results obtained by the administration of identical psychological tests in highly divergent cultural settings. Examples can be found to bear out the feasibility of such comparisons, given due consideration for cultural differences in the content of par-ticular items. In most instances, however, one finds that in-surmountable difficulties are involved in any attempt at translating individual items of objective questionnaires or structured tests for comparative use between literate cul-tures. As a consequence, those who are working in the field of psychodiagnosis have learned to delimit the use of such questionnaire or objective methods very carefully in instances where individuals come from divergent cultural backgrounds.

The Rorschach is the only projective test that has been applied in enough different cultural settings to permit a comparative assessment of its validity for cross-cultural analysis.

Administration of the test is simple. The respondent is given the ink-blot cards, one by one, and asked to tell what he sees. His responses are recorded by the test-administrator. When he picks out small details of the blot, he is asked where he sees them. Thus it is possible to compare his responses with those of other people, and to tell whether his perceptions are com-mon or uncommon ones.

Since the scoring system is objective, it is easy to compare the frequencies and the ratios so obtained for one cultural group with those for another group. But the real problem comes with attempts to interpret the Rorschach scores.

One of the early cross-cultural studies for example, was made by Bleuler and Bleuler (1935) who tested twenty-nine adult Moroccan farmers. They obtained a super-abundance of small-detailed responses. The Moroccan ratios of responses to the total blot, to details in the blot, and to small details were 2.4 to 7.8 to 7.9 respectively, while the average of these ratios among Europeans for total plus detail to small detail is be-tween 5 and 15 to 1. For instance, the Moroccans might see a man's head in a small detail no more than one millimeter in diameter, while ignoring the total blot. This kind of response among Europeans indicated schizophrenia. Did it indicate the same thing for Moroccans? Bleuler and Bleuler suggested that this type of response is characteristic of Arabian mentality— that Arabians are not capable of good synthesis or integration and are lacking in abstract generalizing ability. This interpretation has been challenged by other psychologists and students of cultural differences—so much that Duijker and Frijda (1960, p. 74) conclude that:

> Studies using only one national group and characterizing its members exclusively on the basis of traditional Rorschach interpretation should, in our opinion, be regarded as useless for the purpose of studying national character.

On the other hand, DeVos (1969, p. 341) argues that certain simple cultures lack a "well-disciplined, reality-oriented ego structure" and says that in some cultures, "There is modally present a serious interference with the capacity for reasoned thought when the individuals are emotionally aroused."

In an earlier work, DeVos (1966) calls for a thorough knowledge of the culture by the person who interprets the Rorschach scores. He says:

> Even assuming that there are universals in human nature and carefully observing the distinctions to be made between social adaptation and internal adjustment, before one can hope to use the Rorschach or any other test cross-culturally, one must perforce make some further assumptions about the feasibility of eliciting samples of responses to identical stimuli which can be interpreted with equal validity irrespective of culture. Quantitative testing of validity is very difficult with the Rorschach. The material elicited evades mechanical systems of scoring. Scoring a Rorschach properly demands an experienced interpreter. Both quantitative and qualitative comparisons are possible but only when certain explicit reservations are kept in mind.
>
> Cross-culturally there are extreme variations in the type of responses elicited which gainsay ordinary clinical interpretations based on the usual quantitative scoring methods now in vogue. Nevertheless the Rorschach responses, as Hallowell (1955) justly points out, elicit samples of standardized behavior that can be interpreted in the context of the culture

producing it as well as in terms of an individual's own patterns of thought and perception.

Hallowell's use of the Rorschach in his thorough studies of several American Indian cultures convinced him that the various scoring categories of the Rorschach have a substantial identity of meanings.

An alternative attitude toward the use of the Rorschach is illustrated by the work of Dubois (1944) in her study of the people of the South Pacific island of Alor. She administered the Rorschach test to thirty-seven adults and sent the protocols to the Rorschach specialist E. Oberholtzer for a "blind" analysis. The results of this analysis were combined with data from autobiographies and from field observations obtained by anthropological methods. In this case, the use of the Rorschach was controlled by the anthropologist.

A warning about jumping to conclusions concerning a society is contained in the study by Helm, DeVos, and Carterette (1963) of two neighboring Athabascan Indian settlements in northern Canada: Dogrib and Slavey. Although they have the same sub-culture and are very close together geographically, their Rorschach records are rather different. In Dogrib there is "much more evidence of inadequate reality testing and poor intellectual functioning." The authors ascribe this difference to "genetic or functional family differences."

Gardner Lindzey (1961, pp. 299–300), writing of projective techniques in general, says:

> A defect of many of these studies . . . is the tendency toward mechanical application of scoring systems and interpretative generalizations developed in connection with the study of educated European and American subjects. To most observers, it has appeared that the users of projective techniques have been the strongest resistors to actuarial methods of psychometric procedures. If such were the case, one would expect the interpretation of projective-technique protocols in anthropological research to rely upon various complex and elusive cues, or clinical judgments, entailing the testing context, the individual subject, and a variety of other information. The typical report gives quite the contrary impressions, for we find a willingness to equate a particular type of projective-technique response regularly to a particular personality attribute. Actually, if we remove from this literature all in-

terpretative statements dependent upon Klopfer's specific generalizations, we would probably eliminate three quarters of the results we have examined. . . .

. . . (One finds a) *tendency to take group averages and treat them as descriptive of the group as a whole.* This procedure is particularly prevalent in studies employing the Rorschach test, where many investigators have secured averages from the various Rorschach scores or ratios and then proceeded to develop a psychogram from these group averages and to interpret this average psychogram as representative of the personality of the group. In actual fact the group may include no single member whose psychogram closely resembles the average profile. The essential error in this procedure is its failure to take into consideration the likelihood of wide differences in test performance among the members of a single culture.

DeVos (1966) concludes:

Psychological tests can only with considerable difficulty be comparatively applied trans-culturally. Of the methods of testing now in general practice the Rorschach as a relatively unstructured and economically efficient technique has been put to widest use. This test, a valid though imperfect means of obtaining perceptual responses related to a number of intrapsychic structures, has not always been adequately interpreted nor flexibly adapted to the task when applied cross-culturally. There remains considerable controversy and misunderstanding as to its merits and deficiencies.

As a means of eliciting standardized evidence of mental functioning and psychological defenses or controls, the test supplied valuable evidence that cannot be readily obtained by other methods. It must, however, not be interpreted out of context but must be used in conjunction with other data in respect to the social environment. Of itself it cannot uniformly predict the overt appearance of what is socially perceived as disturbed behavior.

Holtzman Ink-Blot Technique

Well aware of the problems in using the Rorschach test in cross-national research, Holtzman (1968a, p. 136) developed an ink blot technique as "a new projective method designed to overcome psychometric limitations in the Rorschach." Besides including more rich and varied ink-blots there are differences between the Holtzman Ink-blot Technique (HIT) and the Rorschach in administration and standardization which make the HIT more amenable to cross-national utilization.

Rather than give as many responses as he wants to or can give, the subject taking the HIT is asked to give only one response per card. By thus holding the number of responses constant, a potentially-contaminating cross-national variable is eliminated. Subjects in different cultures may by virtue of cultural strictures or tradition vary greatly in the number of responses they would or could give to inkblots. This fact could cause considerable difficulty in comparing scores of countries which vary on this dimension.

Immediately following each response, the examiner makes a brief inquiry about certain aspects of the response to obtain additional information helpful in scoring. Three kinds of questions are permissible in the standard administration: a question to clarify location, a question regarding characteristics of the percept, and a general question encouraging elaboration. Standardization of instructions and standard behavior of test administrators is vital in cross-national studies but difficult to attain. Brief, simple, and clearly delineated probing, as described by Holtzman, is clearly an advantage of the HIT over the Rorschach in research in general and certainly so in cross-national research.

"Carefully matched, parallel forms of the HIT are available, permitting the use of test-retest designs and the study of change within the individual" (Holtzman 1968a, p. 136). The additional advantage here is finding those cards which are particularly discriminating or popular in various countries, because there are sufficient numbers of cards (Knudsen *et al.* 1966).

Group administration of the HIT has been thoroughly investigated and proven feasible and highly desirable for cross-national research. (Swartz and Holtzman 1963). The directions, both written and verbal, for group administration of the HIT are standard. For cross-national research purposes the group method should greatly decrease the variability due to examiner which would be greater in individual administrations both within and between countries. The economy of group administration cannot be overlooked in planning any sizeable cross-national research.

Interpreting and analyzing cross-national data with this instrument should be facilitated by the use of the standardized percentile norms provided for twenty-two variables on a number of U. S. populations. As work continues on the longitudinal study being conducted by Holtzman and Diaz-Guerrero *et al.* (1968), norms will undoubtedly be developed for Mexican subpopulations as they are compared with the U. S. children and the U. S. norms. As the HIT is used in other cultures, additional comparisons using the twenty-two standardized variables will be carried out.

Standard scoring systems, which are recognized to some degree within the profession, have been the accepted methods of scoring the Rorschach, and now the HIT, in research studies in one or many nations. As long as we bear in mind that particular variables do not necessarily have the same meanings and same intercorrelations with other personality and behavioral indices across countries, the information from studies using these scoring systems can be useful. This caution constitutes one of the hard-earned realities culled from the history of experience with the Rorschach.

Another method developed for use with the Rorschach has not been employed with the HIT. With suitable modifications, the Symbolic Analysis or quantitative content analysis developed by DeVos (1952) for the Rorschach could be used. DeVos (1961) has used his method with interesting results in American, Japanese, and Algerian populations. The criticism often aimed at the conventional scoring systems of the Rorschach in cross-national work might also be directed at the standard scoring method of the HIT. The DeVos method eliminates much of this criticism, has good cross-national interpretability, and should be applicable to the HIT.

Drawing Tests

In this section we will discuss the use of drawing tests as projectives for use in cross-national studies, and other uses of drawing tests. The Goodenough method will be discussed elsewhere.

Machover's (1949) presentation on the projective aspects and interpretation of human figure drawings inspired much clinical and research work. Machover presented hypotheses about the structural and formal aspects of drawing, a basic so-called "body-image" hypothesis which holds that persons asked to draw a picture of a person actually draw pictures of themselves, and detailed hypotheses on the meaning of drawings of different types of the various parts of the body. Swensen (1965, p. 650), in a devastating review of the literature since Machover's book, concludes:

> Machover's hypotheses concerning the DAP have seldom been supported by the research reported in the literature. . . . It is suggested that the opinion of clinicians that the DAP is of value as a clinical instrument, despite the lack of experimental evidence to support this judgment, is due to the fact that the DAP, in a few cases which impress the individual clinician, does provide an indication of the nature of the individual client's problems.

Hammer (1965, 1968) attempts to combat the effects of Swensen's arguments by pointing out the rarity of extreme deviant signs which do not show themselves in sufficient numbers to provoke significant differences in research studies, and by alluding to the intricate and multifaced sides to self which can be projected into drawings. He makes a strong case for the clinical use of the technique (1968, p. 385) and illustrates "that in the hands of some . . . projective drawings are an exquisitely sensitive tool, and in the hands of others, those employing a wooden, stilted approach, they are like disconnected phones."

Unfortunately "exquisitely sensitive" scoring systems which are dependent on the personal expertise, empathy, and intuition of the scorer are not practical in cross-national research. Scoring of this type is fraught with so many problems that the scoring methods which Hammer would probably consider "wooden, stilted" are sought as the answer to reliability problems. Swensen discusses the difficulties of establishing reliability with the Draw-a-Person technique. The data are limited and conflicting. Hammer, in effect, acknowledges the problem of establishing reliability by pointing out the great individual variability in using the technique. An example of such a scoring method which has been used cross-nationally with good results is Swensen's sexual differentiation scale (1955). Rabin and Limuaco (1959) achieved high scorer reliability ($r = .90$) with a reduced version of Swensen's scale.

Rabin and Limuaco's study illustrates the use of a drawing technique to test a specific cross-national hypothesis. This tactic is suggested by Swensen in his critique, i.e., that specific hypotheses relating to the interpretation of drawings, and particularly Machover's interpretations, be tested as the next step in research on and with drawing tests. Rabin and Limuaco (1959, p. 211) predicted "on the basis of reported differences between the differentiation, . . . that Filipino children will show a higher degree of sexual differentiation as measured by a scale designed and adapted for this purpose, and based on the Draw-A-Person test. . . . The obtained differences supported the hypothesis at a very high level of confidence." The five point scale of sexual differentiation they used was:

1   Little or no sexual differentiation (the two drawings are practically not differentiated from one another).

2   Poor sexual differentiation (some differences in length of hair and body contours are present).

3   Fair sexual differentiation (clearer differences with respect to the items in the previous category as well as additional secondary sexual characteristics).

4   Good sexual differentiation (including clothing, proportions, and more subtle facial characteristics).

5   Excellent sexual differentiation (consistency in the differentiation in every respect).

This scale is simple, easy, reliable, and directly applicable to their hypothesis. In order to learn more about the drawing tests and interpretations from them, and to study cross-national differences reliably with understanding, limited, exact, "wooden, stilted" scoring systems are required. When Machover's hypotheses have been clearly tested in various countries we will then be able to make cross-national comparisons using or rejecting her hypotheses.

Another approach to the use of human figure drawing techniques has recently been employed by Dennis (1966). Dennis's (1966, pp. 2, 4) thesis is that children's drawings of human figures reveal their social values.

> When we say that drawings of a man reflect group values, we are referring to the content of the drawings. We are not re-

ferring to their size, or to the pressure upon the pencil, or to erasures or firmness of line, but to the kinds of men drawn, that is, whether they are soldiers or farmers, bankers or beggars, and so forth. Our proposal is that children generally draw the men whom they admire and who are thought of favorably by their societies. . . .

. . . In other words it is our hypothesis that drawings do not merely mirror the environment. They reflect values or preferences, not the frequencies of experiences.

The main portion of Dennis's study consists of male drawings from boys from twenty-seven groups in the following countries: the United States, Mexico, Great Britain, Sweden, West Germany, Greece, Turkey, Lebanon, Israel, Iran, Cambodia, Japan, and Taiwan. Analyzing the 2550 drawings Dennis (1966, p. 172) concluded:

Although boys draw only men of whom they have some knowledge, either real or pictorial (that is, they seldom create imaginary men), among the many kinds of men with whom they are acquainted in life or in art, they most often draw men who represent the positive values of themselves and their respective societies.

Dennis was not content with the chapter in his book which dealt with the religious content of drawings. For all the children studied, regardless of their religious background, Dennis found little or no religious content. According to the book's theoretical position the interpretation is that the children place little value on religious symbols, persons, or activities. Dennis and Uras (1965) explored this problem further in a study which illustrates this technique. To establish the validity of his finding with children, Dennis felt he had to show high religious content in a group that one would assume had high religious values. He looked at drawings by 100 nuns and found seventy-four drawings with religious content. This high percentage of drawings with religious content establishes that in groups where religious values are prevalent these values will show themselves in the drawings of the group.

Drawing techniques have been used primarily in three ways. The first, to study "intelligence," is discussed elsewhere in this volume. The second, to assess individual personality, is discussed above. We see potential value to the method but caution that Machover's hypotheses are untested, and the clinical approach is not applicable in cross-national studies at this time. Through systematic research over time justifiable interpretations may be established. The third use of drawing tests is the value testing approach used by Dennis. This new approach has great merit as an easily applicable, clearly interpretable, method of testing values cross-nationally.

Chapter 4

Other Instruments

THIS CHAPTER DISCUSSES A VARIETY of instruments used in cross-national research. Our discussions do not include all instruments that have been or could be used in cross-national studies; rather we have attempted, particularly in this chapter, to provide the reader with examples of techniques for investigating cross-nationally a variety of areas from social psychology.

Essays on Vital Subjects

Essays on Vital Subjects is a vague category of instrument which has been used in cross-national research. The three types of this instrument we will examine in this section illustrate the simplicity of instruction and specificity of task which makes this technique particularly applicable. The scoring methods associated with these instruments originated from the data they procured. Content coding systems were informally applied. The difficulty of predicting the types and range of responses cross-nationally increases the usefulness of scoring systems built on a study of the data.

Critical Incident Technique

One Vital Subject method, the Critical Incident Technique (Flanagan 1954) has generally been used in an interview format. However it appears to be equally useful as a written technique and has been used cross-nationally (Dennis 1957a). When using this method the researcher asks the subject to describe one, two, or several instances of specific kinds of behavior. For example, Dennis (1957a) asked subjects to describe instances when they had been praised, in an attempt to discover what is rewarded and therefore valued behavior in culture groups in Lebanon. The incidents were categorized into broad categories: Academic, Assistance (to a specified other), "Good" Behavior, Sports, Giving or Sharing, and Creative Work. Dennis found highly significant differences between the American and the Near Eastern groups, and much similarity among the Near Eastern groups. Dennis (1957a, p. 438) concludes:

> On the basis of our experience the Critical Incident Technique is recommended to psychologists, anthropologists, and others as a useful tool in making cross-cultural comparisons. Its usefulness, of course, is not limited to studies of praise.

Essay on the Future

Gillespie and Allport (1955) used both a questionnaire and an autobiography in their study "Youth's Outlook on the Future." In the list of requirements for a cross-national survey they include, "uniform and comparable instruments which, even when translated, convey the same meaning to the subjects" (p. 4). This requirement is easily met in the autobiography instrument. With an introduction and some suggestions for proceeding, the instructions are, in essence, "beginning at the present, write a few pages concerning your expectations, plans, and aspirations for the future" (p. 41).

Presumably Gillespie and Allport were assured by their colleagues that the instructions had the same meaning in their native language as they had in English. Certainly on the face of it, translating these instructions so that they are comparable in other languages presents no apparent difficulty.

The scoring of this instrument is again by content coding. Gillespie and Allport make considerable use of the data produced by the subject as an example and the reader is able to "feel" closer to the subjects as a result of reading their productions.

Reliability is a particularly difficult achievement with this type of an instrument, but Gillespie and Allport have met the problem in a practical way. In order to test reliability one cannot split into two halves what is really a single item. A retest on a single item would give the respondents time to consider a task that they could easily remember, destroying the important factor of spontaneity. Gillespie and Allport developed a questionnaire which covered the various demographic information they wanted plus a range of questions which theoretically considered attitudes central to a youth's view of the future. To a great extent the same factual information might be gathered from the two instruments. To the degree that they do coincide on areas where the subject covers the questionnaire material in the autobiography a tentative reliability is determined. Although the authors do not utilize this feature of their design, their inclusion of the second instrument to test the same variables is a particularly valuable approach to cross-national investigations.

The Person I Would Like To Be Like

Every person creates for himself an ideal self, or an ego ideal. The ideal self of the child depends upon his experience with other people. As the child grows his experience with people broadens, and he discovers new values in them. Consequently his ideal self changes and develops.

Most children can speak readily about the ideal self if they are asked direct questions such as: What kind of person would you like to be when you grow up? From as early an age as six or seven, most children answer this question readily, and they continue to do so as they grow through adolescence. Accordingly, the study of the development of the ideal self can be accomplished simply by collecting essays on this topic.

Studies of this kind have been made in the United States for the past sixty years. Although the questions asked have not been identical, they have been enough alike to permit comparison, and thus it is possible to trace changes in the ideal self according to the decade in which a person lives, as well as according to the person's age.

The developmental schemes are similar in societies with a basically similar family structure and with a similar level of urbanism and technology. However, some differences can be traced to differences in culture. Studies made by the same method in the United States, Argentina, and New Zealand do show differences (Havighurst *et al.* 1946, 1965; Havighurst and MacDonald 1955). However, age differences and social-class differences within a given society seem to account for more of the differences than national differences do.

The North American studies show a development with age in the way a person describes his ideal self. Commencing with age six or seven and continuing through age nine or ten, nearly all children name the parent of their own sex as the person they would like to be like. Occasionally a grandparent or an aunt or uncle is named, but this can usually be explained by the fact that this person has been especially close to the child and has acted as a parent-substitute.

The sequence of categories of the ideal self is as follows:

P Parent.

S Parent-substitute or parent-surrogate. A grandparent, aunt or uncle, or occasionally a teacher.

G A glamorous adult. A person with a romantic and ephemeral fame, much in the popular view because of qualities of appearance or conduct more or less superficial: stars of cinema or television, athletes, characters in popular fiction, people in exciting occupations such as astronauts.

H Heroes. Persons with a secure claim to fame, which has been tested by time. A few living people may be assigned to this category—such as a great scientist, a great humanitarian like Dr. Schweitzer (during his lifetime), a great statesman, or a great artist.

St. Saints or other religious personages.

A Attractive adults known personally to the subject. In general these are young adults in the neighborhood, older brothers or sisters, or young aunts or uncles.

C Composite or imaginary characters. In general they are abstracted from a number of real persons, but they may be completely imaginary.

M Age-mates. Companions of nearly the same age.

O Occupation only. Sometimes a subject simply states the occupation he wants to follow, such as *carpenter* or *lawyer*, with no mention of other characteristics.

NC   Not classifiable in any of the previous categories. In general this reflects a rejection by the subject of the idea that he should want to be like another person. Often the subject writes "I want to be myself, and nobody else."

These categories have been listed in the order of their appearance by age, though the categories appearing least frequently do not have any obvious relation to age after about age ten (e.g., S, H, St., M, O).

There is no problem of reliability of scoring this essay, though there is little or no evidence concerning the test-retest reliability of this instrument. As for validity, the essay has obvious face validity, and no other validity test has been applied.

Measuring Values with This Essay

It is possible to analyze this essay in terms of the values expressed by the writer. The directions usually read as follows: "Tell something about this person's occupation, appearance, how old he or she is, what he or she does with free time." The result is usually an essay of five to twenty lines, which can be subjected to content analysis. Dorr (1951) employed this method in the Prairie City Study with ten- to eleven- and sixteen- to seventeen-year-olds. Several categories of values can be identified, and groups from various countries or social classes can be compared.

Summary of Essay Instruments

Although constructing instruments of the "Essays on Vital Subjects" category is not an easy task, it is easier than constructing many other kinds of instruments and as worthwhile. The rule of thumb may simply be: If you have a question to ask which is not only of theoretical importance but of some cross-national importance and applicability, ask it. Dennis wanted to know what behaviors were valued in various cultures so he asked young people to tell him when they were rewarded, using the Critical Incident Technique. Gillespie and Allport wanted to know what youth expected, aspired to, and planned for in the future so they asked for autobiographies including this information. Havighurst wanted to know what the ideal self of youth was in different countries at different times, so he asked them to tell him about "The Person (They) Would Like To Be Like."

"Essays on Vital Subjects" are not deep probing psychological instruments. If certain specific behaviors, which do not carry negative connotations in a culture, are important to a theory, it is assumed that by asking questions about them one can elicit the needed information. If specific attitudes or opinions are of interest, again a researcher simply questions his subjects about them. The degree of reliability and validity characteristic of the instrument depends on the rapport the examiner establishes with the subjects and the experience and trust the subject has toward the tests and the examiner. The traditional methods of testing reliability are virtually impossible with this type of instrument. Using two methods to test the same variables, a form of convergent validation, is the most useful way of establishing the reliability and validity of the instrument in each case.

The instruments examined here are only a few of the possible established instruments of this type. Hard work and careful pretesting will aid construction of other tests of this type to fit individual research interests and needs.

Informal Interview Methods to Study Moral, Emotional, and Cognitive Development

Piaget's Stories.

Since 1930 systematic research has focused on the child's moral and emotional development and his development of concepts about the real world around him. The leader in this research has been Jean Piaget, a Swiss psychologist. He proposed a broad theory linking the child's growth in knowledge with his experience with the people who are mentors and models and with his experience in the world.

Piaget used informal interviews with Swiss children, often with stories which he asked them to explain or interpret. Thus he elicited a wide variety of idiosyncratic responses with which he worked inductively, finding categories which fitted the responses. This method is easy for anthropologists, and for social psychologists who do not feel a need to use highly standardized and quantitative methods, people who are likely to study cultural differences. The problem for the social psychologist has been to get enough comparability of field procedure and data analysis to allow him to make reliable comparisons from one cultural group to another. Thus the critical points are sampling and reliability.

Attempted replications revealed that the growth processes he described did exist, in general, but results did not accurately fit his early findings. Piaget says that he expected this result, since the development of the child's mind depends on its interaction with the social environment and will therefore vary as the social environment varies. Piaget is an environmentalist with a view of the child's mind as an active, searching process by which he comes to terms with the world around him.

Animism and Immanent Justice

According to Piaget's theory of moral development, all children grow up in an atmosphere of moral constraint in which they think of punishment as issuing from all-powerful and all-knowing sources. These sources may be parents or other people in authority, or they may be supernatural forces. The child does not at first make the distinction between the natural and the supernatural or the living and the nonliving.

In a modern society the child's "moral realism" (the belief that morality is imposed by an unchangeable and unchallengeable external set of moral forces) gradually diminishes as he experiences social and moral relations with other children where his own voice counts; as his reasoning power increases; and as he is subjected to the moral theory of adults around him. He learns a theory of cooperative morality—of justice that works through reasonable human beings; of punishment that depends on wrongdoing being discovered and judged in relation to the intentions of the wrongdoer (except, of course, for the punishment that comes from the individual conscience).

Piaget suggests that the child's moral development will take a different course in a "primitive" society. Such a society will make children more rigid in their moral theory as they grow older and will exercise more moral constraint on them. If this society has a world view which includes a supernatural power that watches over men and rewards and punishes their actions, then belief in immanent justice will probably be as strong or even stronger in older children as in younger ones. (Belief in immanent justice is the belief that there is a power in the world which punishes people for wrongdoing through its influence over "natural" things and events. The phrase "immanent punishment" is used by some writers instead of "immanent justice.")

Investigating the concept of immanent justice sometimes leads to an investigation of animism, or the belief that things other than animals and plants are alive. The Chicago Study of Indian children (Havighurst and Neugarten 1955) used a story similar to one used by Piaget (1932) and to variants used by Lerner (1937) and by Dennis (1943). The story was as follows:

Story: This is a story about two boys. These two boys, named Jack and Paul, were out walking, and they came to a melon field. Each of them stole a melon and ran off to eat it. But the owner of the field saw them and ran after them. He caught Jack and punished him, but Paul got away. The same afternoon, Paul was chopping some wood, and the ax slipped and cut his foot.

Questions:

A Why do you think Paul's foot was cut?

B If Paul did not steal the melon, would he cut his foot?

C Did the ax know that he stole the melon?

The reliability of the answers to this test was studied in three ways: by making an inquiry at the end of the test interview, by repeating the test in the native language, and by comparing the answers to questions A and B. Havighurst and Neugarten came to the conclusion that much individual variation exists—an individual child will sometimes change his answer when the test is repeated—but the results for a group are stable and reliable enough to serve as a base for generalizations on group averages.

Further information on the validity of this procedure for measuring belief in immanent justice and in animism is provided by Jahoda's (1958) replication of the Chicago Study with children in Ghana, West Africa. He found much less belief in animism and in immanent justice than had been found in the studies of American Indians. Jahoda doubts that there is actually much difference between the West African and the American Indian youth. Looking at a number of studies made by various methods in various primitive and modern societies, he concludes that the apparent results are due to the methods used both to question the children and to analyze the responses. He believes making a global assessment of the child's belief based on the entire interview is better than treating quantitatively the answers to specific questions. He says (p. 245), "There is an inherent arbitrariness in any assessment of the incidence of immanent justice, which no refinement of mere technique would be able to overcome." With respect to the study of animism, he concludes (p. 211), "One is faced in this sphere with an inherent and inescapable relativity of all findings: numerical frequencies are necessarily a function of the particular method of assessment employed; and cross-cultural standardization is likely to be no more successful than in the case of intelligence tests."

Our view is that with careful attention to the difficulties presented in the published studies, a researcher or a cooperative research group making comparative studies in several cultural groups can achieve reliable results.

Moral Ideology and Rules of Games

Two aspects of the development of moral judgment can be usefully studied cross-culturally. One is the attitude of respect for rules—the essence of morality—and the other is the actual substantive content of morality—what behavior is good and what is bad?

Piaget (1932) proposed a theory of the development of moral judgment which made a distinction between "morality of constraint" or "heteronomous" morality, and "morality of agreement" or "autonomous" morality. In the stage of morality of constraint, children accept rules from outside authority and consider rules absolute and unchangeable; they later progress to a stage of morality of agreement, in which they learn to make rules for themselves by common agreement among those who are involved. A child develops from the level of heterono-mous to that of autonomous morality as a result of his social experience with age-mates, who are his equals—in contrast to his parents and other adults, who gave him his first rules. Through the give-and-take of play with age-mates, the child learns that rules are man-made and can be changed by agree-ment of the players. He generalizes this to cover other rules, including the rules of moral conduct. Thus he comes to feel personally responsible for morality, because he participates in the process by which moral rules are made.

In his book Piaget suggests that the attitudes of children toward rules in primitive societies should *not* show a develop-ment parallel to that in a modern society. This suggestion is expanded in an unpublished lecture by Piaget at a seminar in Paris (1947).

> In so-called "primitive" societies the economic division of labor is unknown; and as a consequence so also are individual psychological variations, "social classes," and conflicting ide-ologies. The sole fundamental differentiation known to them, apart from sex, is that of "age-groups":—childhood, adoles-cence (including initiation), young adults, mature men, and the "Elders" who are the true heads of the tribe. The Elders have authority over all the lower age-groups, but, far from being freer than the young, they are themselves abject slaves to the will of the spirits, to that of their ancestors, and to the traditions linked thereto. Thus the dominant note in such a society is the constraint exercised by earlier generations over their successors, and this "gerontocratic process" explains why the individual is progressively less free as he grows older.

Piaget's theory was tested with American Indian children in the Chicago Study by asking them questions about rules of games. Havighurst and Neugarten (1955, Ch. 5) found that the Indian youth did not show the steady growth from moral heteronomy to moral autonomy that we expect in children of a modern society. They found that the Navaho children from an isolated, unacculturated area made a distinction between rules of games they had learned in school, such as basketball, and rules of the native games they learned at home. An eighteen-year-old Navaho boy who had gone away from his isolated home to an Indian boarding school, speaks about football and says that "the coaches or head people" get together and change the rules. Concerning Navaho games he says that rules cannot be changed "because the holy people taught us them. It is not right to change them."

The games of the white culture are learned in school from teachers or from older children. The Indian children have the usual experience of white children with respect to the rules of these games. Rules are changed or adapted to local conditions: size of play space, type of equipment, and so forth. The games of the native culture are not taught to children, in the sense that actual instruction is given, but rather they are observed until prospective players feel sufficiently sure of their skill and grow audacious enough to try. The games are an integral part of the culture of the adult society. The native games are allied with the religious beliefs and the world view of the Navaho. Every game has its legendary origin, told over and over on winter nights around the fire.

A simple procedure introduced by Bavelas (1942) and adapted by Havighurst and Neugarten (1955) may be useful in studying the moral ideology of children of different cultural groups. The child is told by the tester, "I want to find out what boys and girls of your age think are good things to do and bad things to do." Then the following questions are asked while the tester records the answers on the test booklet:

---

1. What could a boy (girl) of your age do that would be a good thing to do, so that someone would praise him (her) or be pleased?

2. Who would praise him (her) or be pleased?

3. What is another thing, a very good thing, that a boy (girl) could do so that someone would praise him (her) or be pleased?

4. Who would praise him (her) or be pleased?

5. What is still another thing, a very, very good thing, that a boy (girl) could do so that someone would praise him (her) or be pleased?

6. Who would praise him (her) or be pleased?

These questions regarding "good things to do" and "who would praise" are asked each subject at least three times and more often if the subject talks freely. Then the child is asked:

1   What could a boy (girl) of your age do that would be a bad thing to do so that someone would blame him (her) or think badly of him (her)?

2   Who would blame him (her) or think badly of him (her)?

These questions were asked at least three times of each Indian child; more frequently in cases where the child responded freely. The instructions to the white children in Midwest were as follows:

Put your name and age at the top of a blank sheet of paper.

We are interested in finding out what boys and girls of different ages consider good things to do, and what they consider bad things to do. This is not a test. Any answer you give is correct, but the best answers are what you *really* think. A "good thing to do" or a "bad thing to do" might be at school, at home, at work, at play—anywhere.

What is something a boy or girl of your age could do, which would be a good thing to do, and which would be praised or approved?

Who would praise or approve?

Midwest children were asked for nine "good" things and, by rephrasing the question accordingly, for nine "bad" things. Thus Midwest children gave a total of eighteen responses, compared with a total of six responses from Indian children.

A similar procedure was followed by Havighurst (1954) in a set of studies of children and adolescents in New Zealand. The responses were placed into categories by the researcher. With sixty-two categories, three judges agreed on the categories for 180 respondents in 97 percent of the responses. On a test-retest study with white midwestern children in the fifth and sixth grades, the correlation coefficient for frequencies in each category of behavior mentioned was .91 for girls and .86 for boys.

There are substantial differences in the behaviors mentioned as *good* or *bad* between the various tribal groups of Indian children, and between the white children of the American Midwest and the white New Zealand children. There are also differences in the "surrogates"—the people cited as praisers and blamers for good or bad behavior.

Attitude Development

The development of a wide variety of social and personal attitudes among children of different cultures can be studied in two ways: first, by studies of attitudes toward specific persons or institutions with the Semantic Differential or with direct attitude inventories; and second, by a kind of global attitude questionnaire or interview which invites the respondent to describe his attitudes. This latter method has been used by anthropologists in exploratory work and has been adapted by the Chicago Indian Study group in the form of the *Emotional Response Test* (Havighurst and Neugarten 1955, Ch. 3 and Appendix B). The test format can be interview or questionnaire.

Question: Sometimes people are very happy. Have you ever been very happy?

Answer:

Question: Can you remember when you were very happy? Tell me about it.

Answer:

Question: Can you remember another time when you were very happy? Tell me about it.

Answer:

Question: Can you remember another time when you were very happy? Tell me about it.

Similar questions were asked for sadness, fear, anger, and shame. Then the subject was asked, "Tell me, what is the best thing that could happen to you?" Finally, the subject was asked, "What is the worst thing that could happen to you?"

This procedure was adapted for the white children in Midwest. There the subjects were tested in classroom groups, and they wrote their own responses. The administrator made the following statement:

We are interested in learning more about the lives of boys and girls, or young people, so as to compare their experiences with the experiences of people in other cities or other countries. Therefore, we would like to have you tell us a little about your experience. Will you please take a piece of paper and write down on it three things that have made you happy? You can write anything you please. These things might have happened a long time ago or they might have happened recently.

Now write the word "sadness" on your paper, and under it tell about three times when you were sad. Tell what it was that made you sad.

Now write the word "Fear" on your paper and tell about three times when you were afraid.

Now write the work "Anger" on your paper and tell about three times when you were angry.

Now write the word "Shame" on your paper and tell about three times when you were ashamed.

Now write the words "Best Thing" and tell what is the best thing that could happen to you—not the best thing that has happened to you in the past, but the best thing that could happen to you in the future.

Now write the words "Worst Thing" and tell what is the worst thing that could happen to you.

The responses are placed in categories by the researcher, and the frequencies of the various categories compared.

It is immediately clear that language will be a problem for cross-cultural comparisons. How are the words: *happy, sad, afraid, angry,* and, above all, *ashamed,* to be translated? There is no unequivocal translation for the word or concept of "shame" in some languages. Some lean toward *embarrassment* and others toward *guilt.* Generally, the Indian children gave responses indicating embarrassment, while the Midwest white children gave responses indicating guilt. Here, we are dealing with the fascinating problem of the nature of the superego or conscience in various societies. Leighton and Kluckhohn (1947, pp. 105–106) comment:

> Control of the individual is achieved in Navaho society primarily by "lateral sanctions" rather than by sanctions from above. That is, the Navaho from childhood on is brought into

line more by the reactions of all the people around him rather than by orders and threats of punishment from someone who stands above him in a hierarchy. "Shame" is the agony of being found wanting and exposed to the disapproval of others, as opposed to the fear that some single superior person will use his power to deprive one of rewards and privileges if specified tasks are not carried out according to instructions.

Navaho sensitivity to "shame" likewise largely takes the place that remorse and self-punishment have in preventing antisocial conduct in white society. Navahos do not lie awake nights worrying about the undiscovered "bad" things they have done. Because they have not internalized the standards of their parents and others elders but, rather, accept these standards as part of the external environment to which an adjustment must be made, "divine discontent" is an emotion foreign to the normal Navaho. It is believed by some that "progress" occurs in societies of the Christian tradition largely because each socialized individual is trying to avoid the self-reproach that would be incurred by failing to live up to the ideals inculcated in childhood. Navaho society is (or would be if not under continual pressure from white society) much more static, since "shame" ("I would feel very uncomfortable if anyone saw me deviating from accepted norms") plays the psychological role which "conscience" or "guilt" ("I am unworthy for I am not living up to the high standards represented by my parents") has in the Christian tradition.

The reliability of the Emotional Response Test has been studied by a test-retest of Midwestern white children with an interval of two years. Coefficients of correlation between the two administrations when based on comparison of frequencies by category range from .95 to .59. The lower coefficients suggest that comparisons between groups should be made only when the smaller group has as many as forty members.

It would be useful to study the validity of this test by the method of comparing two or more tests which purport to measure a given emotional attitude.

Non-Verbal Intelligence Tests

The comparative study of intelligence by means of tests has been a popular but frustrating problem throughout the present century. Until about 1930 it was generally assumed that racial differences in intelligence are genetic, and, therefore, a comparative study of different racial groups with intelligence tests would reveal the basic genetic differences between races in intelligence. As the belief of social scientists in genetic group psychological differences waned, while evidence of environmental influence on intelligence and other psychological tests accumulated, a set of questions arose about the meaning of racial differences and of national differences in average scores on the tests. Furthermore, after 1940 evidence accumulated that different social classes in a modern society showed different characteristics on psychological tests. That such differences could be genetic was dubious, in view of the great mobility and mixture of marriages in this country which tend to make the genetic composition of various social groups equal.

One possible reaction to this ambivalence is to stop making comparative studies of intelligence and related characteristics among socioeconomic, national, and racial groups, on the assumption that no innate difference among the groups in these traits is possible despite what the tests say.

Another alternative selected particularly by those who use intelligence tests is to make a variety of comparisons using many testing procedures. Then the group differences that are observed are supposedly related to differences in the experience of one group or another with the items and procedures of the tests. Results show that those tests which depend on reading, and those which test knowledge of words and word meanings are clearly unsatisfactory for a study of groups with different levels of literacy. Furthermore, for literate groups who speak different languages the problem of translating the tests from one language to another and retaining the same level of intrinsic difficulty is severe.

As a result nonverbal performance tests of "intelligence" have been developed that can be used with people of varying degrees of linguistic sophistication.

The Wechsler Intelligence Scales for adults and children have been widely used in English-speaking countries and adapted for use in other languages. Some of the subtests contained require reading ability, but most are not dependent on reading. The so-called "Performance Tests" can be used separately from the verbal scales. The Grace Arthur Performance Battery was widely used around 1940 as an individual test that required little or no verbal facility.

In addition to individual intelligence tests, group tests that required little or no reading ability were developed—such as Raven's Matrices, Thurstone's Test of Spatial Imagery, the nonverbal tests of the California Mental Maturity Scale, and the Porteus Maze. It soon became clear that nonliterate groups did quite well on nonverbal tests. It also became clear that groups of people who did not know English well (such as American Indians and Mexicans, scored better on performance tests of intelligence than on verbal tests. A group of Indian or Mexican children in an American school commonly averaged ten or more IQ points higher on a performance test than on a verbal test.

For example, Havighurst and Hilkevitch (1944) reported on the use of a short form of the Arthur Performance Scale with American Indian children of six tribes. The average IQ for a group of 670 children aged six through fifteen in eleven Indian communities was 100.2. A subgroup of thirty Sioux children, who averaged 102.0 on the Arthur had been tested with the Kuhlmann-Anderson verbal group test the previous year with an average IQ of 82.5.

This experience gave rise in the 1940s to several attempts to provide a "culture-free" test of intelligence. The proof that such a test had been produced was to show that a typical middle-class white American group scored about the same as non-middle-class or non-English-speaking groups would score. For a time, it appeared that this might be possible, but eventually the evidence piled up that the middle-class American group was slightly more competent than lower-class groups even in these tests.

Thus the conclusion became generally accepted by 1960, that performance tests of intelligence removed much of the difference between social-class and nationality subgroups which had been found in verbal tests, *but* there remains a set of differences after efforts have been made to control the studies for obvious environmental differences. These residual group differences may be due to undiscovered differences in the experience of the members of the various social groups, or they may be due to genetic group differences.

The Goodenough Draw-a-Man Test of Intelligence

Comparative studies of children from various cultural subgroups with a test that purports to measure intelligence have used the Goodenough Draw-a-Man Test since 1926 when it was first described. The test is usable for children aged six to twelve. It requires only a piece of paper and a pencil and the instruction to "draw a man." The test is scored by counting the number and accuracy of details in the drawing, without reference to the aesthetic value of the drawing except that correct proportions of the body and a profile rather than a front view gets slightly higher scores. The test might be described operationally as one of accuracy of perception, since it is scored for the accuracy with which it represents a man. It might also be called a test of "mental alertness" or attention to the world around the child.

Reliability of the test is quite high, on the basis of test-retest measures. Reliability of the scoring is high. Most scorers, after a little practice and discussion of their procedures, have a product-moment correlation coefficient with other scorers in the neighborhood of .95.

Reliability of the instrument was severely tested in the case of Hopi Indian children examined by Dennis (1943), and tested again by a University of Chicago team (Havighurst, Gunther, and Pratt 1946) a year later. For sixty-three children, the product-moment correlation between the two sets of scores was a disappointing 0.52.

In the case of the DAM, average IQ scores have been reported from 112 to 93 for what appear to be good and fairly large samples in a study of American Indian children in seventeen communities reported by Levensky (1970). A somewhat similar study of nine Indian groups showed a range of average IQ scores from 120 to 103 (Havighurst, Gunther, and Pratt 1946). Dennis (1966a) put together a list of forty studies of as many groups, with mean IQ scores ranging from 125 to 53. His explanation for these differences proposes that groups scoring high will come from societies which have a high development of representational art or are high in respect to exposure to modern visual media. He attributes the relatively low scores of Muslim and some Arabian-Jewish subjects to a traditional religious bar against making images of men. Other low scores he attributes to isolation from modern media of mass communication and the two low group scores of 56 and 53 (from Syria and the Sudan) to lack of experience with pencil and paper as well as minimal exposure to representational art.

Studies of correlation between the DAM and other intelligence tests show low and quite variable results. Havighurst *et al.* (1946) reported product-moment correlation coefficients ranging from .10 to .64 between DAM and Grace Arthur IQs for five Indian groups. Kennedy and Lindner (1964) tested black children from southeastern USA with the DAM and an individual Stanford Binet test, getting correlation coefficients ranging from .59 for first grade pupils to .29 for fourth grade pupils. Harris (1961) reported a correlation coefficient of .22 between DAM and Raven Matrices scores. Khatena (1964) found a correlation coefficient of .26 for school children in Singapore between DAM and Raven Matrices.

In conclusion, no test of intelligence is known which is free of cultural influence; consequently, cross-cultural comparisons should not be interpreted in terms of genetic superiority of one group over another in intelligence. They should be interpreted as indicators of cultural differences, though the cultural characteristics to which they are related are not all clearly known.

The Cornell Medical Index

Many intensively studied variables in comparative cross-cultural investigations are obviously related to the health and vigor of people; health, however, is seldom measured. Researchers tacitly assume it remains constant over the various samples. All subjects are "ambulatory;" none is confined to an institution. On the basis of such criteria they report a normal distribution of health and vigor.

These assumptions are clearly inadequate when comparative studies consider mental health, job competence among older workers, attitudes toward retirement, etc. However, valid measures of physical health and vigor are difficult to achieve without a medical examination, and even medical examiners hesitate to make global judgment of the physical health and vigor of groups of people.

In the hope of getting reasonably good measures of health and vigor for use in large-scale questionnaire studies of adults, the Cornell Medical Index was developed (Brodman *et al.* 1951, 1956), which consists of 195 questions about physical and mental health. This self-report correlated fairly well with ratings made by medical doctors on the basis of medical examinations. Consequently it has been used as an instrument for a health survey. Schneider and Streib (1969) used it in their study of the relations between health and attitudes toward retirement among elderly American workers, but this research did not raise questions of cross-cultural validity.

An adapted form of the Inventory was used with Alaskan Eskimos by Chance (1962). He was concerned with three questions:

1 To what extent were Eskimo "concepts" of health and disease similar to those of American culture;

2 If the concepts were similar, could the "terminology" of the questionnaire be revised so as to secure reliable and valid responses from Eskimos and still retain comparability between Eskimo and United States responses;

3 By what "method" could the data be most objectively obtained?

Through studies made by Public Health Service personnel, it was established that Eskimos on the Arctic Slope of Alaska, residing in the Point Barrow area, were making much use of the services of the U. S. Public Health Service, and had undergone a major shift from traditional Eskimo disease-beliefs to those of western medicine. Native curers have largely disappeared.

The Questionnaire was adapted by omitting a few questions not medically pertinent to the Eskimo environment, and by revising the terminology of other items to fit Eskimo custom. For example, the question, "When you catch a cold, do you always go to bed?" was changed to, "When you catch a cold, do you always have to take it easy?" since Eskimos rarely go to bed with a cold.

Three young Eskimo adults were employed as survey interviewers, and they employed English or Eskimo as the situation required. The survey of an entire village was completed in three weeks. Some of the questionnaires were compared with medical records at the Barrow hospital and found to agree sufficiently to justify the use of the questionnaire.

However, in a few instances cultural factors strongly influenced Eskimo responses to the questionnaire items. One major factor produced substantial differences between Eskimo and average American responses. This was the Eskimo's tendency to withstand physical illness with little or no complaint and to insist on going on with his workload. Hence the question, "Does sickness often keep you from doing your work?" was answered positively by far fewer Eskimos than by North Americans in general. Chance (1962, p. 417) concludes:

> While the high degree of conceptual equivalence in most areas of the questionnaire warranted a continuation of the investigation, the preliminary study clearly illustrated the fact that before a foreign health survey instrument can be used comparatively, one must first have a detailed understanding of the attitudes of the group in question and the cultural matrix to which these attitudes relate; and second, one must provide appropriate translation not only of the instrument's terminology, but its conceptual underpinning as well. Unless these two cautions are kept clearly in mind, the validity of any cross-cultural study of health and disease may be strongly questioned.

A similar attitude is probably responsible for difference between the responses of older British, Danish, and American people to "How would you rate your health—good, fair, or poor?" in the study by Shanas *et al.* (1968). Interviewing national samples of people over sixty-five, and excluding persons who were bedridden, researchers found that elderly people in Britain, both male and female, were more likely than elderly people in Denmark and the United States to say that their health is good. These findings were not anticipated, since evidence indicated a greater physical incapacity in the British than the other two groups. Perhaps the British character, with its tendency to "keep a stiff upper lip," suppresses the tendency to complain about poor health.

Thus it appears that differences in self-report on health and vigor between different cultural groups may represent real differences in the state of health, or differences in attitude toward physical illness. Only more extended knowledge of the cultures concerned can provide a valid interpretation of self-reported differences.

Word Associations

Word association tests investigate group differences and similarities, and therefore are theoretically amenable to cross-national research. The most popular instrument in research of this type is the Kent and Rosanoff Word List (1910) which emphasizes the frequency and comparability of meaning of the "primary responses" (the most popular responses) in the various groups being studied. The most recent standard for determining primary responses is the work of Russell and Jenkins (1954), "The Complete Minnesota Norms for Responses to 100 Words from the Kent-Rosanoff Word Association Test." The original frequency tables are in A. J. Rosanoff's *Manual of Psychiatry* (now out of print). The "standard" Classification of Reactions can be found in the Examiner Manual of the Kent-Rosanoff Free Association Test printed by C. H. Stoelting Company.

People interested in word association are usually also interested in language. They are theoretically people who would take careful note of translation difficulties and the subtle differences in the meanings of words across cultures, both cultures defined by national boundaries and language differences and cultures within the same "language community" differing in country or social class. In fact, the people carrying out word association studies have been particularly sensitive to translation problems both in preparing their instruments and in the analysis and discussion of their findings.

This sensitivity is illustrated in the cross-national work of Rosenzweig (1961) and that of Moran (1966). These works indicate both the traditional approach to word association research and its current evolution.

Rosenzweig administered the Kent-Rosanoff list to French, German, Italian, and American samples and compared their primary responses for meaning. He found "a strong tendency for primary responses to corresponding stimulus-words to be equivalent in meaning" (p. 359). In another type of analysis he found that "when both stimulus- and primary response-words were adjectives or when the response was opposite in meaning to the stimulus-word, there also was high agreement among languages."

Rosenzweig accounts for some of the differences he found by noting an approximate number of inexact translations between languages, and peculiarities of individual languages which cause disagreements such as "when the primary response in one language was one of completion, i.e., a complex of which the stimulus-word is a part" (Rosenzweig 1961, p.

359). A sensitive treatment of the language difficulties not only adds value to the study, but also makes it a model from which anyone working cross-nationally can learn.

Moran (1964, 1966) employs the notion that some subjects in the "free" word association experiment will respond predominantly with one "category" of association. Four such "categories," or idiodynamic associative sets, have been developed: Perceptual-referent (predication), Object-referent (functional), Concept-referent (synonym or superordinate), and Dimension-referent (contrast or coordinate). These sets constitute usual association patterns for certain individuals. Moran and Murakawa (1908), in a comparative study of data from Japanese, American, and Mexican people, found the same four sets extant in the three countries. They report (pp. 179–180):

> Just as interesting as the cross-cultural similarities in idiodynamic associative sets are the extreme differences in proportions of the set types in the . . . cultures. Both the generality of these four different association structures and their variable incidence in different populations appear to create serious problems for the traditional account of how words acquire hierarchical associations with other words.

The issue here is whether culturally popular responses are uniformly related to the popularity of the responses among individuals or whether the popular responses are an artifact of the frequency of the associative sets of individuals within a population. Moran suggests that the instructions given can differentially elicit either the popular responses or the individual associative sets, and he refers to the work of Ach (1964) and that of Horton, Marlowe, and Crowne (1963).

From this rather small sampling of work from word association research two important positive implications for cross-national studies emerge. The first concerns the whole theory of language in relation to cognitive behavior, the Sapir-Whorf hypothesis. Language affects cognition and thereby attitudes, values, and personality; and as cultures differ in language, a problem of all cross-cultural research is identified: to what degree are the similarities and differences found between cultures the result of cultural, social, and psychological variables and to what degree are they evidence of far reaching cognitive mediated language differences? Some clues to a resolution to this question may lie in the future of word association research on idiodynamic associative sets.

The second implication is methodological. Sensitive handling and concentrated analysis of the denotative and connotative meaning of the "same" words in various languages is well illustrated in this type of social psychological-linguistic research. Using the Semantic Differential for his research, Osgood (1960, p. 168) hypothesized the generality of connotative phenomena across languages while stating that denotative differences correspond to "the multitudinous and arbitrary sets of correlations between perceptual events and linguistic events (i.e., the 'rules of usage' of any language code)." Although Osgood concedes that only limited but consistent evidence supports his hypothesis, in conjunction with the word association findings and methods, his hypothesis bodes well for the cross-national researcher. He holds that, with care, items can be constructed which carry the same connotative meaning in different languages.

Word association findings, and particularly those of Moran, signal a warning for users of social psychological instruments. When constructing or using instruments which call for one or several words as completions or associatives (such as in the Sentence Completion or the Uses Test) idiodynamic associative sets must be considered. Differences found with instruments of this type may in fact result from taping the same associative mechanisms as the word association procedure. It would seem therefore that variety of stimulus structure is warranted. A sentence completion stem such as, "Work is_____," is similar to asking for an association with the word "work." Cross-national differences on a stem such as "Work is_____" may really be only association set differences. If the stem is changed to "Work, in my opinion, is _____" the association tendency may be weakened, and the desired data elicited. However this is pure hypothesis.

This discussion has pointed to an area with substantial cross-national potential both as a substantive research area and as a model of linguistic sophistication and technique.

Social Distance Scales

Since the publication of the original article in 1925 the Bogardus Social Distance Scale has remained consistently one of the most popular tests of social attitudes in the literature. From Bogardus's (1928) major research on race attitudes in the U. S. and a multitude of subsequent studies in the U. S. by numerous researchers to the recent work of Triandis and Triandis (1962), the Bogardus Social Distance Scale, expanded, modified, statistically calibrated for equal intervals, or altered to accomodate varying cultures, has shown its usefulness in national and cross-national studies.

The original Bogardus Scale listed the following instructions and column headings (the points on the scale):

According to my first feeling reactions, I would willingly admit members of each race (as a class, and not the best I have known nor the worst members) to one or more of the classifications under which I have placed a cross:

1   To close kinship by marriage.
2   To my club as personal chums.
3   To my street as neighbors.
4   To employment in my occupation in my country.
5   To citizenship in my country.
6   As visitors only to my country.
7   Would exclude from my country.

Campbell (1952, p. 324) evaluated the Bogardus Social Distance Scale:

Appropriate for measuring social distance (acceptance or rejection) toward racial, national, religious, occupational, or other definable social groups. Suitable for use as a group test for adults and children down to the sixth grade. Attitudes toward twenty or so groups can be assessed in ten to twenty minutes.

With LeVine in 1965 Campbell shows twelve studies in which the Bogardus scale has been used in countries other than the U. S. These studies date from 1935 to 1962.

This literature supports some universal generalizations: that all ingroups, as judged by the average member, hold most outgroups at some degree of social distance, even if not that all ingroups hold all outgroups at some degree of social distance. Over and above these universals, perusal of the literature shows large differences among ingroups in the degree of social distance at which outgroups are held, and for any ingroup, highly stable differences in the distance to which different outgroups are held. These dimensions of variation are among the most important of those on which social-science theories offer predictions.

The degree of intricacy that is possible using this technique in cross-national research is illustrated in the Triandis and Triandis (1962) study. Their Greek and American student samples rated imaginary people with different combinations of racial, social class, religious, and national characteristics. Questionnaire and other personality and attitude scale measures were taken. Stimuli were selected and data analyzed using factor analysis. Differences between and within the samples as well as similarities were found which were

> incorporated into a theory of prejudice which was suggested in Triandis and Triandis (1960) and which utilizes conformity to group norms, cognitive dissonance produced by value inconsistencies, and insecurity of the individual as some of the key variables (p. 20).

The Bogardus Social Distance Scale or variations thereof have proven value in cross-national research. In order to better understand the determinants and effects of social distance, and the relation between varieties of social change and changes in social distance attitudes, cross-national studies using this method are highly recommended.

Visual Perception Tests

Theoretically and methodologically cross-cultural studies of visual perception illustrate the rationale for cross-national research. The investigations by Rivers (1901) are considered the first of this type of study. Rivers presented a variety of visual illusions to native islanders while on the Torres Strait expedition. He compared their responses with the norms of western respondents, finding differences in susceptibility to some illusions, with the natives less susceptible on some, no differences on others, and the natives more susceptible on one. These differences were to be used for a long while in evaluating the nativistic-empiricistic conflict.

The nativistic-empiricistic controversy assumes that as responses are universal across cultures they are nativistically based, whereas empiricistically based responses would vary systematically across cultures. Allport and Pettigrew (1957, p. 104) define these terms a follows:

1   The nativistic, i.e., theories emphasizing the role of retinal and cortical functions relatively unaffected by learning, habit, experience, or meaning; and

2   The empiricistic, i.e., theories giving primary weight to the role of experience and learning.

This controversy, although relating here to visual perception, underlies much cross-national social-psychological research.

Allport and Pettigrew, studying the perception of movement, do not attempt to test the efficacy of either the nativistic or empiricistic positions. Rather they attempt to show the effect of "object connotation (meaning)" in relation to nativistic or cumulative habit determinants in the perception of movement. They conclude (p. 113) that "an adequate theory of perceived movement must therefore allow a place for the subject's specific assumptions of meaning even though it cannot be based solely on this foundation." No current theory, nativistic or empiricistic can completely describe perception without some explanatory assistance from the other.

In a study of fifteen societies, Segall, Campbell, and Herskovits (1963, 1966) investigated the pattern of response differences in the perception of geometric illusions. Their findings corroborated Rivers's. They explain these differences as emanating from different habits of perceptual inference which are related to visual environmental factors in the cultural and ecological environs of the subjects. Both the traditional explanation of importance of angularity in urban environments and an ecological explanation relating to probability of seeing lines in a horizontal plane in open, flat, forested, or mountain regions are suggested as factors in responding to illusions. The researchers (1963) conclude:

> Whether or not the correct environmental features have been isolated, the cross-cultural differences in susceptibility to

geometric illusions seem best understood as symptomatic of functional differences in learned visual inference habits.

Visual perception studies consider illusions, perception of movement, and pictorial depth perception, with the bulk of evidence supporting an empiricistic basis for differences. The dimensions underlying the empiricistic differences are becoming more clearly defined. However the nativistic-empiricistic controversy has not been resolved in this area, as the work of W. Hudson (1960, p. 207) from the National institute for Personnel Research in Johannesburg, South Africa attests. In a study of depth perception of school-going and nonschool-going blacks and whites in South Africa Hudson concludes:

> The findings on the black samples are more difficult to understand adequately on cultural differences alone. The process of pictorial depth perception is not beyond the capacity of the black man, but it is a skill in which he has a good deal of leeway to make up. Both cultural and genetic factors play their role in the process.

The differences between cultural groups on visual perception tasks most often result from methodological problems and considerations. As important as this research is in its own right, it sheds considerable light on the issue of instrumentation in all types of cross-national research. Particularly in construction and interpretation of projective instruments knowledge of purely perceptual differences is essential to understanding that portion of the revealed differences which are projective in nature. Both Dennis (1951) and Biesheuvel (1958) suggest that perceptual differences between cultures need to be established prior to constructing projective tests for these cultures or at least at some point so that this information can be used in interpreting the projective materials. Clearly the presentation of the same visual stimuli to different cultural groups cannot be understood social psychologically if the groups perceive the stimuli differently in the first place and the investigator either does not know this or does not know to what degree this is so.

The study of visual perception is not only an enlightening area of research for the study of human differences but also constitutes an essential adjunct technique for improving the validity of projective instruments.

Interviews

The interview method is widely used to obtain factual biographical information as well as data on attitudes, values, and personality characteristics. Since the interview has so many possible variations, it is widely used for comparisons between groups of people within a society and for comparisons of different national and cultural groups. There are two broadly different types of interview and interview methods—the rigorously closed questionnaire interview, and the open-ended interview which encourages the respondent to make idiosyncratic responses. The problems and possibilities for the two types are quite different.

The Pre-coded Fixed-Questionnaire Interview

In this form of instrument, the responses are objectively coded and quantitatively scored. Public-opinion surveys as well as studies which seek to determine facts about health, income, housing, socioeconomic status, educational level, educational aspiration, and sociopolitical attitudes rely upon this instrument. The form may be a questionnaire which is distributed to be answered by the respondent without further interaction with the researcher, or an interview situation, where the interviewer is available to clarify the meanings of certain items or to probe further into one or another area where the first responses of the respondent are inadequate.

Since the responses on this instrument are coded and scored objectively, reliability of scoring is no problem. There may be a problem of consistency of response over time, though this has not usually been considered important.

Problems of Translation. Where an interview schedule is used with people who speak different languages, it is essential to convey the same questions, with the same nuances of meaning in the various forms. For example, a cross-national study of people aged sixty-five and over was made by three competent social scientists living in the three countries under study,

Shanas, Townsend, and Stehouwer (1968), by means of a questionnaire-interview with a carefully designed random sample of people in Great Britain, Denmark, and the United States. The authors, all familiar with the English language, commenced with an interview schedule in English, then translated and adapted it for use in the three countries. They tried this technique in their respective countries and compared their experiences. Framing the questions for connotative equivalence proved to be a difficult task; for example, a question about health asked, "How often do you get dizzy spells?" The British for the word dizzy was decided to be *giddy*, since the word dizzy had another connotation. The Danish word was identified as "svimmel."

The team of researchers held fourteen meetings and exchanged hundreds of letters in order to arrive at truly comparable results. A good part of their work lay in coding the answers to the small number of "open" questions which did not permit an answer that could be automatically placed on a punch card. A large number of the free responses had to be collected and categorized by the three researchers. When they were satisfied that they had seen examples of all the categories of response, they then drew up rules for placing their responses consistently in the categories which had been defined.

It seems probable that comparison of public opinion survey data taken from various countries is sometimes done without sufficient attention to the details of the translation for connotative equivalence.

The Open-Answer Interview Schedule

Another form of interview is often used when the researcher wishes to study widely and deeply the rather complex areas of human behavior and experience. This is an open-ended, free-response set of questions which encourage the respondent to express his knowledge and attitudes fully and freely. Here, the interview consists of a set of questions designed to open up an area and to get the respondent to speak freely about this area. The researcher takes down as much of the response as possible, or he uses a tape recorder.

In a study of middle-aged and elderly people in the Kansas City area, Havighurst (1957b) asked a carefully selected sample about their favorite leisure-time activity. The respondent was asked to describe what he did, where, how often, and what values it had for him. In this way an abundance of information was obtained in a form which could not be simply transferred to a punch card. However, it was desirable to quantify these data if possible, and Havighurst and his colleagues (1957a) worked out a set of *rating* scales which could be applied to the interview material with high reliability. Thus they were able to compare people of different social class, age, and sex.

Administration of the Open-Answer Interview. The Open-answer interview depends upon a well-trained interviewer to phrase appropriate questions to elicit the kind of information desired. The interview schedule is divided into areas, with a few leading questions to open up the respective areas. The interviewer then invents further questions, or "probes" until he feels that the respondent has told as complete a story as is necessary for the research.

For this procedure the interviewer must be coached by reading other interviews, discussing the purposes of the interview, and finally, trial interviews in which he goes over the interview in detail with his research supervisor. Thus the interview instrument is the trained individual rather than the printed form interview schedule.

Where the success of the interview depends heavily upon cooperation and understanding between the respondent and the interviewer, the personality of the interviewer is an important factor, and interviewers are selected accordingly. Also, where the interview is conducted with respondents of various nationality, race, or social class, it may become important to employ interviewers of the corresponding group; for example, in the National Study of American Indian Education, directed by Havighurst (1970a), interviews were conducted with students, parents, teachers, and influential people in the community under study. As a rule, the research staff interviewed the students and teachers, while local people were employed and trained to interview parents and influential people, generally in the tribal language.

Analyzing and Scoring the Open-Answer Interview. In order to quantify the data from this type of interview, the interview must be analyzed, and its contents placed into categories or on scales which can be treated mathematically. In this way an interview can be quantitatively compared with other interviews.

Analysis into Categories. Responses may be placed in categories which have no necessary relationship with one another. For instance, if the respondent is asked to name his favorite leisure activities, his responses may be placed into categories such as: handicrafts, games, observing sporting events, fishing, gardening, watching TV, etc. Then the frequencies in the various categories may be compared for various groups of persons. This procedure is fairly simple, depending mainly on the creation of meaningful and useful categories, which cover all or nearly all of the responses that are given.

Analysis with Rating Scales. An interview sometimes measures the respondent's attitude, status, or competence on one or more scales of intensity or extensity. With scores on such scales, people of various age, sex, social class, race, or nationality group can be compared. This involves the creation of *rating scales* and establishment of their reliability and validity.

Creating a rating scale starts with the interview schedule, when the areas to be studied are determined. Usually there are several rating scales for each area of investigation, each scale based on a combined conceptual-empirical analysis of the interviews. For instance, if the interview involves attitudes toward religion, the rating scale may be defined conceptually as a scale extending from complete rejection of religion to the opposite extreme of complete acceptance of religion. The researcher reads a number of interviews to find what attitudes are actually operating in his sample. Each interview he reads can be placed on the continuum he has defined. As he reads more interviews, he is able to define points on the scale and to illustrate these points by example from his interviews. Eventually he has from three to nine points (usually) defined by actual statements from interviews. He decides how many points he wants on his scale, and sets it up accordingly, defining each point on the scale and often illustrating each point with quotations from interviews.

Such a scale does not necessarily have equal *intervals* between each pair of points, as would be true of a scale for measuring height or weight. But the points defined on the scale are in order of size, from the least to the most of what is being measured.

Reliability of a Rating Scale. *Raters* or *judges* who hear or read the interviews make the actual ratings. Then the judgment of these people determines where a respondent's answer is placed on a given rating scale. The rating process is never as objective as using a meter stick or a weight scale to measure height or weight. But the rating process can be made quite reliable or consistent if the rating scale is good, if the interviews give adequate information, and if the raters are trained to use the rating scales objectively.

The reliability or consistency of ratings is discussed by Guilford (1954), Edwards (1954), Kendall (1955) and other statisticians from the point of view of statistics. Their statistical procedures are applied to cross-cultural or cross-national interview studies by researchers who have used interviews. The procedure used by Froehlich (1969) and by Havighurst (1970a) is described here, as an example.

The act of placing the information from an interview at a point on a rating scale requires the rater, or judge, to do the following:

1   To understand the dimension that is being measured by the rating scale.

2   To discover the information in the interview that is relevant to this dimension. This includes reading carefully the responses to the questions most explicitly relevant to the dimension that is being measured; and also picking up clues from other parts of the interview that throw light on this dimension.

3   To hold himself strictly to the evidence from the interview—to avoid possible "halo effects" due to other information given by the respondent concerning his good or bad qualities as a person.

4   To avoid any tendency to be overgenerous or overnegative in his behavior as a judge.

Most people can learn to follow this procedure by practice and criticism from themselves and others. Only a few operate with prejudices, stereotypes, and "blind spots" so much as to invalidate their work as judges. Nevertheless, the best procedure is to use two or more judges or raters for all interviews, and to average their ratings. In the rare case when they disagree considerably, they can discuss their ratings and one or the other generally finds that he is mistaken. Where they differ only one or at the most two points on a scale of six to nine steps, the average of their ratings is taken. It is well to use raters of different sex or different race or different age in order to avoid unconscious bias or to take advantage of special insight one member of the team may have for certain interview material.

In a major cross-cultural or cross-national use of interviews with rating scales, it is necessary to determine and to report the reliability or consistency level of the ratings. Methods for doing so have been described in the case of a cross-national study of adjustment to retirement by Froehlich (1969) and Bengtson (1969), and in the case of a cross-cultural study of American Indian education by Havighurst (1969).

In such studies there are generally several cooperating research teams, who do the field work in the various countries and cultures involved. To use ratings from their interviews comparatively, they follow this procedure:

1   Create an interview schedule and train interviewers to use this schedule in substantially the same way.

2   Create rating scales that are thoroughly discussed and understood by the members of the cooperating teams.

3   Interview samples of people representing comparable categories in the various research centers or sites, and representative of the populations that are being studied.

4   Establish the reliability of the rating procedure within each cooperating team.

5   Establish the reliability of the rating procedure between the cooperating teams.

The first three steps are accomplished through cooperation of the various research teams (six for the cross-national study of retirement and seven for the Indian study). The following outline of procedure was then followed in the Indian study, and a parallel in the study of retirement.

Each research team selected fifteen to twenty interviews that covered the range of interviews they had made—age levels and sex of students, experience and sex of teachers, age and degree of contact with the white society for Indian parents. Members of the teams had previously read interviews and made tentative ratings; they then discussed their ratings and ironed out differences of procedure and judgment among themselves. Two or more judges then rated the interviews, without discussing their ratings.

The degree of reliability or consistency of the ratings was measured by the following:

1   Product-moment coefficient of correlation between pairs of raters among the k raters.

2   Kendall's coefficient of concordance (corrected for ties of ratings among the subjects) computed for the k raters (Kendall 1955).

3   The intra-class correlation coefficient computed for the k raters (Edwards 1954, Guilford 1954). This is an analysis of variance procedure which compares the variance among k raters for n interviews with the variance of the ratings among the n interviews.

Methods b and c produce similar reliability coefficients. The product-moment correlation coefficients show which judges are least in accord with the other judges.

This procedure measured the intracenter reliability of the ratings for each dimension on each interview. When the reliability was low, the cause was either faulty work by one or more judges (who were then instructed to practice and improve their ratings, or were removed from the rating process) or inadequate data from the interviews, in which case the dimensions with unreliable ratings were discarded from the Study. When the intracenter reliability had been established in this way, the intercenter reliability was similarly studied by selecting three widely-differing interviews from each of the seven centers (n = 21 interviews) and by asking each team to rate all twenty-one interviews. The average or modal rating from a team on each dimension of the twenty-one interviews was taken as the rating for that team. (The team became a single judge for this purpose.)

If the intercenter comparisons showed a particular center

to be "out of line" it was so informed, and its ratings on its own interviews were not used for comparisons with other centers. Actually, the intercenter reliability coefficients were high on most of the dimensions for all the types of interview.

Validity of a Rating Scale.   The question of *validity* of a rating scale based on an interview is not often discussed critically. The question is not whether the rating scale gives a *valid measure* of the data from the interview, but whether the interview provides a *valid report* of the respondent—his behavior, status, personality, etc. The interview is a self-report, and is open to questions of validity that apply to all self-reports. The interview has the advantage, generally, of being extensive and intensive, giving the respondent adequate time to present himself fully and giving the interviewer opportunity to ask questions to clear up apparent contradictions or to involve the respondent in contradictions if he is fabricating.

One of the most difficult of all interviews from the point of view of validity was the Kinsey (1948, 1953) Study conducted with individuals about their sex life. Even though his respondents were explicitly willing to tell him about their intimate sexual behavior, it seems likely that some of them would omit or alter certain details. Yet many critical examinations of Kinsey's data and his methods have led a variety of potential critics to the conclusion that his interviews were essentially valid, and probably far more valid than a self-report questionnaire would have been, without benefit of an interviewer.

Our view is that the interview method is potentially the most valid method there is for getting a self-report on material of which the respondent is conscious and about which he does not feel a deep need to falsify. But the interviewer must be skillful, well trained, and able to relate well to people. And quantification must be obtained through the definition and application of categories or rating scales.

Part Three

Sampling in Cross-National
Research

Chapter 5

Sampling

"MOST CROSS-CULTURAL STUDIES by American psychologists consist of unsystematic replication of American research in another literate society. . . . The theoretical rationale for undertaking the cross-cultural study in the first place is often conspicuous by its absence" (Holtzman 1965, pp. 68–69). Fortuitous circumstance has probably been the main determinant of what measurement techniques to use in the society under investigation. A psychologist visiting another country to teach, travel, or research tries out an instrument, or instruments, in which he is interested. Two or more researchers from different countries, who are acquainted, who have been collaborators on other work or have studied together, who are friends, find an area or issue of common interest and arrange to investigate it "cross-culturally." Since research originating in this way has provoked studies which have been carried through easily, congenially, and inexpensively, it will no doubt continue. And as sophistication in and knowledge of cross-national methodology becomes more widespread, these researchers should continue more productively.

In designing research great care and deliberation goes into the choice of variables. In designing cross-cultural research care should go into the choice of the culture variable, which is, after all, as amorphous and unwieldy as any variable one could choose.

We ideally assume that the selection of the variable and the theory to be tested precedes the selection of the cultures in which to study them. (Although in actuality the selection of

157

cultures most often is prior, in which case the logic of the following argument should be reversed). With the theory, the variables, the basic design, and the research question, i.e., the basic design requirements, established, the choice of culture variables (cultures, countries, nations in which to test) is most simply based on the selection of cultures as similar or dissimilar (contrasting) on a specified variable or variables.

When the countries chosen are as similar as possible, the differences found between them on the investigated variables are difficult to explain except as the countries differ. That is, a comparative study of, say, occupational aspirations in Peru and Chile may reveal differences on these variables between the two countries. Certainly these differences would be pinpointed on variables like social class, region, etc. Yet the general national differences between these two countries is much smaller than between either and the U. S. A. or either and Japan. The religious, historical, political, and linguistic similarities are great. The cross-national differences found in such a study could be attributable to subcultural differences, or to variables that may not have been controlled.

When the countries chosen are as dissimilar as possible, the differences found between them on the investigated variables are difficult to explain because of the great number of uncontrolled variables. An investigation of occupational aspirations between Germany and Nigeria would produce a multitude of differences. Relating and comparing the differences by social class, tribe, geographic mobility, social mobility, rural-urban, traditional-modern, and historical-cultural dimensions could explain some of the differences between the countries but would be extremely difficult and expensive. So at either extreme the problems are great.

When the purpose of the study is to describe a culture on specified variables or to replicate a study in another culture, one culture might be as good as any other. Studies of this type will become increasingly valuable when a number of rigorous replication studies have been completed in a number of countries and are available for systematic comparison.

When the intention is to compare two cultures, whether they are similar or contrasting, inferential explanation in terms of the relationships between independent, dependent, and cultural (whether dependent or independent) variables is all but impossible. The most one can do is fully describe each of the two cultures and describe the differences between them. From the perspective of a data bank being developed in the literature, two-culture study data would have to be classified as descriptive also. One cannot confidently speak of changes in attitudes, values, personality characteristics, etc., in relation to economic growth, geographic region, cultural background, etc., when two cultures are under investigation. In effect, a two-culture study can only be a descriptive comparison.

In order truly to test relationships across cultures, three or more cultures must be investigated. By systematically selecting cultures which are similar on many variables and contrasting on others, relationships and changes can be seen. Suppose one wanted to investigate the relationship between occupational aspirations and expectations and economic development (as measured by national average annual family income) among the lower socioeconomic class. For a three culture study, the strategy would be to select countries with low, medium, and high average family income. Nigeria, Portugal, and the United States, respectively, would fit the low, medium, and high categories. But there would be a multitude of uncontrolled differences between these cultures. Rather, one should choose three countries from the same gross cultural area which range from lowest to highest on the economic indicator. Peru, Mexico and Puerto Rico rank approximately from low, to medium, and high in average family income among the Latin countries. There are many similarities in language, history, and culture among these countries. Differences still exist, such as in the political situation, stability, and educational opportunity. However, by minimizing the differences unrelated to the research question while maximizing and possibly informally scaling the relevant differences between countries, questions of relationships and changes that cannot otherwise be raised can be asked and answered.

The point we are trying to make is simply that the type and the number of cultures chosen dictate the limits of analysis and interpretation. For the broadest predictability and inferential analysis, relationships between at least three cultures must be studied, as in this last example. In any event the purpose of the cross-national study in question suggests the "known" relationships between the cultures chosen as a sample. If the experimental purpose is to establish the fact of wide cultural differences then contrasting cultures should be used. If one intends to study cultural differences in some specific aspect of human behavior, such as children's development of moral character, coping behavior, or arithmetic achievement, the behavior to be studied is well known and carefully measured. Cultures can then be chosen for wide variation on this behavior or for close similarities, or both. When one wishes to discuss the nature of cultural differences, then two or more fairly well known cultures should be used, with some hypotheses about possible differences. In this situation some purely exploratory "fishing expeditions" might be made to open up areas for research.

Sometimes the intent is to compare two or more cultures—two or more nations, social classes, etc. In this case the cultures to be compared are also well known, and there are thus hypotheses about the behavioral differences among them, i.e., differences in child rearing, in cognitive development, in social attitudes, etc.

The sampling of countries can be determined according to the kind of study that is planned. In any case a careful description of the people being sampled is necessary, and the rationale for sampling them.

In summary studies in one other culture can initially only be descriptive, and studies in two cultures can only be descriptive, and the choice of cultures to be studied are irrelevant since all studies will augment knowledge. At the time when sufficient similar studies have been completed in a number of cultures, the combined data from one and two culture studies can be analyzed together, comparatively and predictively. Until that time, in order to run comparative, predictive studies, we suggest selecting countries for investigation on the basis of as much similarity as possible while systematically contrasting their differences.

Sampling Within Countries for Cross-National Comparison

In any country there are subcultural groups which differ in social and personal characteristics. For example: the two sexes, age groups, castes, social classes, religious groups, city dwellers and rural people. The sample to be studied may be:

a   a representative sample of the whole country;

b   a representative sample of a definable part of the country's population; e.g., males or females, adults or children, city dwellers, people with a secondary school education, members of a particular religious group.

In survey studies this type of sampling may be possible, but in studies which look at individuals in depth, it is seldom possible to study a representative portion of the whole country. Most studies will report on a sample of a subgroup, which should be clearly defined, e.g., males with a secondary school education, children aged ten to fourteen who are in public schools. Some subgroups can usefully be compared cross-nationally, and others not. For example, boys might be compared with boys, but it would probably not be useful to compare boys of one country with girls of another country. Probably the following characteristics should be held constant in cross-national comparisons among modern nations: age, sex, social class, urban-rural residence.

Again, some subcultural groups are so completely characteristic of a particular country that they should always be included in a cross-national study. For example, if one country is almost entirely Roman Catholic, such as Brazil, and another is almost entirely Protestant, such as Denmark, one would include religion as a part of the national characteristics, rather than attempt to compare the few Brazilian Protestants with Protestants in Denmark so as to make a cross-national study holding religion constant.

Religion is a variable to be considered with special care. Sometimes it might be useful to keep religion constant in comparing two national groups. This might be useful in comparing the United States with Holland, where each country has a substantial portion of Catholics and of Protestants. Other times it might be better to get a representative sample in terms of religion in comparing two countries, so that religion is treated as part of the set of national characteristics that is to be compared under the term "nationality." This might be done in comparing Argentina, which is mainly Catholic, with the USA, which is both Catholic and Protestant, while both countries have Jewish minorities. In countries with a large Muslim population, the various Muslim subgroups should probably be identified and the sample defined in these terms.

The general rule concerning characteristics that are part of "nationality" might be that subgroups which appear in substantial proportion in all the countries to be compared should be compared separately. For example, males with males, females with females, while collar workers with white collar workers, adolescents with adolescents. But when a particular subgroup dominates the national sample, such as Catholics in a Catholic country, this characteristic should be treated as part of the complex of national characteristics.

This general rule speaks to the caution stated by Berrien (1967, p. 37), "In the search for similarities, it is necessary to ensure that the differences detected are not the artifacts of inappropriate samples."

Measuring Socioeconomic Status in Cross-National Research

A number of variables relating to occupation, income, education, home type and structure, neighborhood, etc., have been used to calculate socioeconomic status in the United States and elsewhere. Warner *et al.* (1960) describe the basic definitions and rationales for these variables. Socioeconomic status can most efficiently and easily be measured using only two of these variables: occupation and education. This is true within the United States and particularly so in cross-national studies where comparability on the other variables would be exceedingly difficult. Scales have been devised, or are simple to construct, for measuring occupational level and educational level within modern and relatively modern developing countries. In this section we will discuss a method for measuring occupational level, educational level and a combined socioeconomic status level in cross-national research.

Occupational and educational scales are generally six or seven point scales. Each point stands for a variety of jobs or job types or a level of attained education which is considered, for the society in question, to form a natural level of status characteristics and prestige above and below the points lower and higher than it on the scale. Havighurst (1969) relates "It has been shown in studies of occupational status or occupational prestige in many countries that there does exist a rather stable cross-national consensus on the status of most occupations. Thus, Hodge, Treiman, and Rossi (1966) have summarized such studies, and indicated that the correlation coefficient of occupational status measured in any two modern countries is always above 0.9. For instance, Hutchinson (1960) measured occupational prestige among a sample of men in the city of Sao Paulo [Brazil] and found that the scale values correlated 0.92 with the scale values found by Hall and Jones in England."

A scale of occupational prestige exists for most modern countries, or one can be constructed on the basis of sociological studies made in the country. For those that do not, or if the design requires employing the same scale in all countries, one can use a cross-national occupational prestige scale. If the sample includes rural people, a different scale applicable to the occupational prestige of rural occupations may have to be devised. Here again, a cross-national scale may be useful. Following are two International Scales of Occupational Prestige, one for urban and one for rural occupations.

Table 1   International Scale of Occupations

Urban Occupations

1 Medical doctor, lawyer, clergyman, university professor, engineer, owner of a large business or factory, manager of a large business or factory, high military official, high government official.

2 Manager or owner of a business or factory of medium size, accountant, secondary school teacher, primary school teacher with university level of education, commissioned officer in military service from lieutenant to major, journalist, civil servant of executive status, stock broker, insurance salesman.

3 Owner of small business or shop with employees, civil servant of middle level, primary school teacher with secondary level education, traveling salesman, office or bank clerk, trained nurse, laboratory technician, noncommissioned officer in military service from sergeant to lieutenant.

4 Owner of a small fruit or vegetable stand without employees, clerk in a shop, foremen, mechanic, police-

man, electrician, other skilled workers, restaurant cook, conductor or driver of a train.

5   Semi-skilled worker, factory worker, truck driver, waiter, barber, soldier, sailor.

6   Unskilled worker, construction worker, street sweeper, stevedore.

Rural Occupations

1   Landowner with large land area and large numbers of employees for his particular area or state. Does not do manual work on his land. May have a second house in the city.

2   Intermediate, but still rather large farmer of the "gentleman-farmer" type.

3   Small but independent landowner. May do all of his own farm work with machinery or may have a small number of employees. The administrator of a large fazenda or plantation also falls in this category.

4   Small landowner who does his own work. A foreman on a fazenda or plantation also may fall in this category.

5   One who lives on the land of the owner but has his own house, a small land or animal allotment, and shares crops with the owner or gives the owner a certain number of days' work a year: a *meeiro* or *parceiro*.

6   Unskilled agricultural laborer who works for wages and probably does not have a guaranteed income. May live in a village and go out to work by the day. Often lives in a small house provided by the owner on his land.

The rationale for constructing educational scales is like that for occupational scales. The scales will vary from country to country according to the average levels of educational attainment within the countries. Unless an educational prestige scale exists for a particular country, a researcher will have to develop one, according to his knowledge of the social structure of the country. The following examples of educational scales used for three of the countries in the Coping Style and Achievement Study indicate a standard for devising these scales.

USA
1 University graduate
2 Some university
3 Secondary school graduate
4 Some secondary school
5 Primary school graduate
6 Some primary school

Brazil
1 Some University & Graduate
2 Secondary school graduate
3 Junior Secondary school graduate
4 Some Junior Secondary school
5 Primary school graduate
6 Some primary school

England
1 University graduate
2 Some post-secondary
3 Secondary School Graduate
   "A" level, sixth form
4 Some Secondary School
   "O" level, fifth form
5 Left school at fifteen
6 Left school before fifteen

Although in itself occupation is the single best indicator of an individual's status, adding educational level to the scale refines the measure considerably. This is particularly so when information about occupation is scanty. Havighurst (1969) reports

> For example, in the occupations rated 3 and 4, there are a number of positions such as small business man, clerk, salesman, civil servant, which are rather ambiguous, even after one gets a fair amount of information . . . on what the (person) sells, or what kind of office work he does. In this case the rating on education will tend to qualify the occupational score, and thus will help to fix the socioeconomic status.

Since the occupational level is a stronger indicator of socioeconomic status, it is reasonable to weight occupation more heavily in the combined socioeconomic status scale. A usual weighting method is occupational level times 3 plus educational level times 2 equals socioeconomic status. If one is interested in the full range of status groups within the cultures he is studying, he will utilize all levels, or if he is interested in specific SES groups, he will use separate and distinct levels. Children receive SES ranking attributed to their father. Havighurst describes his method for securing equivalent samples of two distinct classes in a cross-national study, applying the method to Chicago and Buenos Aires (1965, pp. 9–10).

The socioeconomic structures of Chicago and Buenos Aires are quite similar.

Sociologists who have studied urban society find that the large cities of Western Europe and of South and North America have similar social structure. Professor Germani, who was trained in Europe, has studied the socioeconomic structure of Buenos Aires thoroughly, and has also served as visiting professor of the University of Chicago. His methods of analysis of social structure are similar to those of Warner which [were] used in [selecting] the Chicago [sample].

The socioeconomic index for the pupils' fathers was based on their occupation and their education. Scales of occupational level and of educational level had been worked out by sociologists W. L. Warner and Gino Germani and their colleagues. These [are] 7-point scales, based on similar concepts of social structure and social status in a modern industrialized community. Both sets of scales were applied and adapted by one of the authors (RJH) who had worked with both Warner and Germani. His aim was to make the scales comparable.

The two educational scales [were similar to those shown above for U. S. A. and Brazil]. Their differences reflect the differences in educational level between the two cities. Chicago men have more years of formal education, on the average, than do the men of Buenos Aires.

For the occupational scales, two existing 'dictionaries' of occupations were used. Each dictionary consisted of a list of occupations with a rating on a 7-point scale for each occupation based on studies of prestige of occupations in the two countries. Germani's (1960) dictionary was made for use in a study of social status of university students. Warner's dictionary was made for use in Chicago in a variety of studies of social status. It was an expanded up-dated version of the scale published in his book, *Social Class in America* (1960).

Ratings for occupation and education were combined with

weights of 3 and 2 respectively, after discussing the question of relative weights with sociologists in the two cities. Thus the socioeconomic index extended in theory from 5 to 35, the lowest scores representing the highest status.

Since it was decided to study two clearly separate social class groups, the upper middle and the upper lower or upper-working class groups, the boundaries of the two classes had to be established on the socioeconomic scale. After studying a few cases of people at the margins of the two classes, it was concluded that the best cut-off points would be 18–20 for the boundary between upper-middle and lower-middle class, and 23–25 for the boundary between upper-lower and lower-middle classes. This would leave out all people with scores of 21 and 22, which are normally held by lower-middle class people, and thus would clearly differentiate the two social class groups in our study. There were also a few exclusions from the Buenos Aires sample of children whose fathers had very high status occupations combined with the highest educational rating. At the other end there were a few exclusions of children whose fathers had the lowest scores in both occupation and education.

Cross-National Comparisons of School-age Children: Special Sampling Problems

When attempting to study school age subjects across nations, a number of sampling problems arise. Some of these problems are unique to the school situation and some relate to usual problems of sampling but are compounded by the necessity of or interest in testing in schools which themselves differ on a number of variables. We will assume that whether one is trying to get a representative sample of all the school age children of a country or of a particular and definable subsample of the school age children of a country, he would be interested in either identifying or controlling the following variables: age, sex, social class, urban-rural residence, and probably ethnicity or minority group, and religion.

Sex and Age. Schools across countries differ in starting age, requirements for entrance and promotion, number of years of compulsory education, uniformity of system (i.e., public schools only, or public, private, and parochial systems), types of schools available (i.e., academic, commercial, normal, etc.), teacher education, coeducational or sex segregated schools, ability or heterogeneous classes, and on and on. These school differences of which these are just a few, but the most noticeable, may be greater within a country or between countries depending on the countries in question. The purpose of this presentation is to indicate the problems of securing the samples on the variables mentioned above in nations divergent on the school system variables mentioned.

The age variable, of unquestioned interest in social, psychological, educational, and developmental cross-national research, presents a number of obvious and subtle problems. The first is whether the age the researcher is interested in is represented uniformly, selectively, or at all in the schools of the country in which he intends to sample. Testing six-year-olds in classroom situations may mean that they have one or two years of experience in some places but will be difficult or impossible in others where schooling does not begin until age seven or eight or where the starting age is not standard. Testing fourteen-year-olds across countries may mean testing students with anywhere from six to ten years of school experience depending on the country. In some countries the fourteen-year-olds will already be a selective group in that dropping out of school may have already begun, or compulsory schooling may have expired, or differential tracks or school types may have selected certain students out of the available sample. Certainly all that applies to the selectivity of fourteen-year-olds increases as one's student sample is older.

In trying to collect data in schools or comparable sex groups the age variable interacts significantly. In different countries the expectations for female education differ both in extent and quality. That means that females will average fewer years of schooling even when the average number of years is quite low by outside standards. It also indicates that females will have diverged from academic careers leading to additional education, into commercial schools that lead to a job or normal schools which lead to elementary school teaching, which may require as few as six or eight years of education. To reach a representative sample of school age children of both sexes in these instances may mean sampling a wide variety of schools and even some children who are out of school, in order to compare the group from one country with that of another where all children are still in school.

The question of coeducation or sex-segregated schools is crucial in cross-national comparisons, where this difference may be unavoidable. Although sex-segregated schools would seem to be proportionately less frequent in public school systems than in private and parochial schools, this is not true in some countries where much of the public education is in the form of boarding schools. So United States researchers may be ill-prepared for the extent of this phenomenon. When both types of systems exist in a country one must choose to sample from one, the other, or both.

The issue in making this decision is the same as in making decisions on all of the variables in question here. First, how does this variable relate to the research question and variables in this study? Second, are the samples between countries likely to be more or less comparable because of your decision? And third, the general rule stated earlier for "nationality" sampling might be applied: if a characteristic of the schools is predominant in a country it should be employed even in comparison with another country where an "opposite" characteristic is predominant; but, if this predominance does not exist, sampling from schools with characteristics that appear in substantial number in each country is open to the choice of the investigator.

Socioeconomic Status.   SES, as it relates to testing in schools, is a very complex cross-national variable. Measuring SES cross-nationally is a separate issue. Here we will look at SES, assuming that our measures are adequate.

Socioeconomic status groups may be segregated into certain schools because of neighborhood segregation and neighborhood schools, or they may be segregated by school systems in that in some countries the upper SES children may attend almost exclusively private schools. On the other hand the school systems may mix the SES groups fairly extensively. If either extreme exists, the sampling problem is negligible in that securing subjects from any one group or all groups will constitute the norm for that group. However, the situation often exists in which some of the children from particular SES levels go to one type of school and others to another. In this situation the researcher who samples from both types of schools must analyze the differences between the subsamples before combining them and treating them alike.

In making the decision to sample from mixed versus segregated SES schools, or from both, the research question and research instruments are crucial. An example of the confounding nature of this decision is the use of a peer nomination technique in the project "Coping Style and Achievement: A Cross-National Study of Children." In Austin, Texas some of the schools sampled were mixed for SES while others were almost exclusively one SES level or another, whereas the schools sampled in Milan, Italy were almost completely SES segregated. When the children were asked to rate the children in their class who were best at task achievement outside of school:

1 This knowledge was different if the children associated with neighbor children of the same SES level but went to school with children from all SES levels, and

2 There was, it seemed, a tendency for the higher SES children to be chosen in mixed classes, while the choice would necessarily be made on individual characteristics when the class was composed of children of the same SES group.

With increased age, school populations will show an increasing percentage of higher SES children, the increment differing across nations. In the United States, in different geographic areas, by age sixteen the upper levels of SES children with few exceptions will still be in school, but the lower SES adolescents will be a selective group in that upwards to 25 percent of these children may have dropped out of school. In Mexico, for example, the vast majority of upper SES level children will probably be in private school, but comparatively few lower SES children will be in school at all, and those that are will primarily be in commercial schools.

Through most of the world an interaction between SES, sex, and age exists in school attendance with a greater and greater percentage of males attending school at the higher SES levels. However, this difference itself is great across nations. A working class girl attending high school and particularly college in Latin America, Africa, and most of Asia is a rarity for her class. In the United States she would not represent the majority of her peers at the college level but would not be as unusual as in these other areas. On the other hand an upper middle class girl in Latin America, Africa and parts of Asia attending university is not as rare as the lower-class girl by any means but is not as common a phenomenon as the upper-middle-class girl on a North American campus.

Residence. Rural-urban residence must be controlled systematically in cross-national sampling due to the great differences found with this variable in a variety of indices throughout the world. The work of the sociologists and demographers is vital in this area in determining what kinds of cutoff points to use in labeling people as rural or urban, and what "urban" means, i.e., small, medium, or large town. Two prominent problems relate to this variable in sampling within countries. One is the question of availability of certain types of subjects, most particularly certain social class levels, and minority groups, and the representativeness of these types when found in urban or rural surroundings. The second is the question of rural-urban migration, which is an important and growing phenomenon.

A couple of illustrations might clarify the first problem. In an attempt to replicate in Puerto Rico a study carried out in Buenos Aires and Chicago, the comparable sampling area selected was San Juan. However, the researchers wished to investigate the variability within the Island as well, which meant sampling in smaller towns and rural areas. The sample in the original study included upper-lower-class and upper-middle-class thirteen- and sixteen-year-olds. Comparable groups were readily available in San Juan and smaller, though medium size (50 to 100 thousand population) towns. Finding an upper-middle-class sample in the rural, central mountain, sections of Puerto Rico was impossible. Using the scale that was designed for measuring status of rural occupations there were no, or so very few, large or medium size farms that a sample of upper middle class adolescents was unattainable. For our purposes this was not a significant problem since we had not intended to compare this area with one where upper-middle-class farm children exist. It would also have presented a problem if one wanted to compare the lower-class rural children with comparable children in an area where they were in mixed SES schools. Another example might be comparing rural-urban ethnic group differences, say for a Jewish sample. Outside Israel one would be hard put to find a sample of rural Jewish children, particularly if he stipulated that they be of European or East European extraction.

The issue of internal, rural-urban migration should probably be considered in cross-national sampling. This phenomenon is prevalent everywhere to some degree and often to a very large degree. In some areas it is a long standing pattern whereas in others it is fairly recent. There are, say in the United States, rural areas which have lost large percentages of their population over the course of the last two or three generations. The population therefore has been highly selected for whatever the relevant variables are that determine internal migration. The cities that have taken in these migrants over two or three generations will probably have second and third generation people throughout the SES range, or at least the bottom two-thirds of the SES range, assuming substantial mobility.

Where this pattern is more recent, and where the occupational and educational mobility is not as rapid as in the United States, both the rural and the urban samples might be quite different from those in the United States. Throughout Latin America, and frequently in India, hordes of lower class rural migrants have settled in and around the major cities. Living in squalid conditions, in shanty towns, oftimes as squatters, they comprise a large proportion of the lower class of these cities. They are new to the city and associate exclusively with each other. The rural-urban differences under investigation in these places might be quite different than in the United States because of the length of history of internal migration on a large scale and because of the social structure which does not facilitate the entrance of new migrants into the life of the cities.

In relation to educational research, the findings within the schools can be very much affected by these differences in the historical makeup of the rural and urban populations, selective migration (to whatever degree that is a valid concept), and the recent history and assimilation of internal migrants.

Just as certain types of students may not be available for sampling in rural areas, so too, certain types of schools and levels of education may not be available in rural areas. In the Cross-national Study of Coping Styles and Achievement, the fourteen-year-olds tested in São Paulo were past the compulsory education limit and therefore a select group, and in Mexico City a large proportion of the fourteen-year-old sample were from private schools. Had we attempted to sample in rural areas in these two countries we would have found that in many areas in Brazil and Mexico no schools are available past primary school, and that children able to attend middle school or preparatory school have to move to their district's capital. When comparing rural children attending "high school," when they have had to move to a boarding school situation, with children living at home and attending compulsory high school, we have a dual confounding of selectivity and the experiences, which we assume are maturing in themselves, of living away from home.

Schools differ in quality of education and quality and quantity of their teachers' education and of their facilities. This fact is obvious in the United States and clearly visible across other countries and within other countries. When sampling in a country which has four or five different types of schools, such as classic, academic, commercial and normal in Brazil, and tremendous differences between the qualifications for students and teachers in rural and urban schools and in public, private, and parochial schools, difficult decisions have to be made about which schools to sample, that is, which schools are comparable across countries. It is also difficult to determine the significance of criteria, such as grades, which are given for different courses between schools and which are administered by teachers with different levels of education and background who, therefore, presumably hold different expectations for their students.

This discussion has raised many questions and supplied few answers. We believe that this approach is, at this point, the safest. No one of the variables discussed can be realistically partialled out from the rest. In sampling children in school, a variety of combinations of these most relevant variables will have to be considered. They will exist in different combinations in different schools in different countries. The problem for the researcher is to control as much of the variation as possible while sampling comparable groups and schools which satisfy the needs of his research question. Knowing beforehand that absolute comparability will not be possible in most instances, the researcher should anticipate differences in his results based on differences within his sample, and should analyze and report his data in light of these sampling differences.

Part Four

Organization of Cross-
National Research

Chapter 6

Organizing an International Cooperative Research Venture

THE NUMBER OF DIFFERENT TYPES of social-psychological cross-national researches range from the large and complex to the relatively simple. We will primarily discuss the more complex study and its organization, but we believe that some, if not all, of the elements associated with the type we will speak of are of value to the other types.

Duijker and Frijda (1960) refer to four types of cross-national study. The simplest is repetitive-successive, which are essentially replication studies. These studies are carried out at one time in one country and later redone in the same way in another country. A repetitive-concurrent study, the second type, is one in which one researcher develops a study to be carried out at the same time by people in other countries. A third type is one in which an international group develops a study to be carried out at various times in their own countries. This type of study is called the joint development-successive type. The final type is called joint development-concurrent, studies in which an international team of researchers develop and carry through, at approximately the same time, a cross-national study.

We will focus our discussion on the joint development-concurrent type, the newest and most rare, the most involved and, we believe, most promising type of cross national research.

They are however fraught with all of the problems inherent in cross national research at this stage in its development.

For the most part our suggestions are based on our own cross-national research experience. We have drawn from the literature for additional ideas on problems and solutions and find much in common with the obstacles encountered and the means employed to dispel them. Particularly illuminating for us has been reference to three joint development-concurrent type researches which have been completed in a number of countries. They are the work of the Organization for Comparative Social Research, the International Project for the Evaluation of Educational Achievement, and the study titled, Authority, Rules and Aggression: A Cross-National Study of Socialization into Compliance Systems.

Preparation

Organization Diagram

The diagram below is of an organizational plan for a joint development-concurrent cross-national study. The diagram is intended to illustrate what we consider the most effective and efficient organization for this type of study: the principal investigators are all of equal rank, so to speak, and all participants, principal investigators and center staff members, are involved both in their own country's tasks (translating, data collection, scoring, etc.) and intercountry tasks (committee, policy work), through a democratic organization.

The rationale and background for this plan are discussed in the following sections.

Participants; Principal Investigators

The decision about participants in a cross-national study should ideally result from calculation and planning. It is a sampling decision whose ideal solution is discussed in the section on sampling between countries. That section refers to the nations from which one samples. Researchers from the chosen countries are the participants in the study.

If all institutions and researchers were interested and able in cross-national research the choice of participants would be

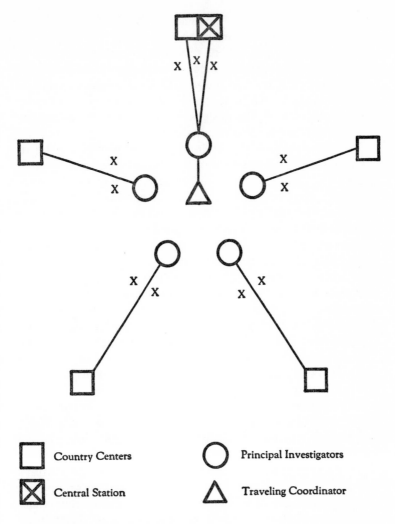

	Country Centers		Principal Investigators
	Central Station		Traveling Coordinator

X   Staff and Committee Members

FIGURE ONE   Organizational Plan for a Cross-National Study

a minor problem. However a number of practical considerations must go into the formation of a cross-national research organization. These same considerations are relevant to preparing a replication study.

In each country one researcher, who is considered to have

the necessary professional credentials, who is interested in the area being studied, who wants to participate, and who, by virtue of nationality, length of residence or extensive study, is familiar with the nation he is to represent, is chosen to be principal investigator for that country. This individual, as principal investigator in his country, assumes dual responsibility for the completion of all tasks designated to his country as well as membership in the cross-national team.

The principal investigator in each country may also be responsible for securing financing for his portion of the investigation. Obviously this can be a severely limiting factor; some countries may not be in a position, for one reason or another, to secure the necessary funding. Some individuals within the country may be able to secure funding whereas others for one reason or another may not be. However, sometimes a single institution may fund the entire project.

If one researcher or research institution secures the money for the whole study, this will usually be the principal cross-national investigator. In all probability the "leader" in initiating the study will continue to serve as the "leader" throughout. The organizational map of the study therefore shows principal investigators from each of the participating countries and a cross-national principal investigator with overall responsibility for the project.

Although one person is designated principal cross-national investigator by virtue of funding, initiation of the project, seniority or whatever, the hallmark of successful cross-national research is democratic organization. Qualified participants from many countries represent not only a variety of cultures but also a variety of academic and disciplinary backgrounds. It is not usually easy to get agreement on points from theory and hypotheses through operationalization and data collection on to analysis and reporting. However in order to work together congenially, and thereby to have all aspects of the study carried out uniformly, full understanding and voluntary agreement to all theoretical and procedural points is needed. There are many ways in which participants and their staffs can be emotionally put off. When this happens efficiency drops, as does communication. A minimum requirement for maintaining good relations between participants is a democratic organizational plan in which all participants feel themselves to be, and truly are, equal.

Centers

The choice of participants will in part be dependent on the resources necessary to accomplish the study and the resources available to the principal investigator in each country. In order to perform the myriad activities that may be part of a country's responsibilities, a certain amount of manpower with varying degrees of ability and experience should be available. Office space and office equipment will also be needed, but just how much will depend on the requirements of the study. Particular people and institutions must be evaluated in terms of potential to successfully perform its part of the study. If this evaluation is positive, the principal investigator in a country with his staff become the Center for that country.

In a joint development study the importance of each individual center is greater than in a replication study. Certainly the task responsibilities must be consummated by the center, but the center is also responsible throughout the study, and especially in the developing stages, for ascertaining whether the plans and instruments are appropriate for their country. Some, if not all, translating is done in the centers. They have to contact schools or agencies or individuals. They must know or be able to find out quickly whether the samples they need are available, whether the approaches to subjects accepted for the study will work for them, whether the subjects will understand what they are to do, whether the questions and problems raised in the instruments are relevant in their area, etc. Pilot testing and statistical analysis will in any event determine the answers to many of these questions. But a good research center team should be able to determine much of this before, rather than after, this work has been done.

When data are coming in, and being scored and analyzed, each center has primary responsibility for its own paper work. The center staff is also responsible for interpreting and correcting inconsistencies and differences between their data, their subjects' interpretations of questions, their own understanding of definitions and variables and what they think the other stations are finding. This is a vital task for each center.

A center has dual responsibility: first, to the project to carry out its assignments, and second to its own data, country, and people, to present accurately the cultural variables influencing the data.

Central Office

Funding and resources will determine where certain tasks are performed. Computer work will be carried out at the center which can most successfully do the work necessary at the most reasonable cost. Other jobs will be distributed to the centers which can most capably handle them.

Since the cross-national principal investigator is responsible for the overall execution of the study he needs a central office which functions to oversee and coordinate the efforts of all the centers. No matter how explicit the instructions and field manuals are for a study, problems and questions arise. No matter how democratically run a project is, quick decisions will have to be made by a single authority. The jobs of the principal cross-national investigator and the central office are like the agencies of government to the legislative and executive branches. The planning and general aims and instrumentation of the study are developed by all principal investigators in conference. The centers attempt to carry out their wishes in exactly the manner specified. When they have questions they refer them to the central office. When they seem not to be doing the tasks as required of them, the central office contacts them. When questions arise at a number of centers the central office either attempts to answer them on the basis of their more complete information, or circulates the questions and attempts to determine the consensus of the centers.

It might appear that a democratically run study should not need a central office which appears to have power that the individual centers do not have. The central office actually should not have additional power, but should act as the facilitator. It serves as a check and reminder to the centers. In this situation almost always some bad feelings rise from the centers to the central station. Some centers will feel that the central office is bullying them, taking too much in its own hands, etc. This organizational problem seems to exist everywhere.

For the central office to do its job most efficiently and cordially it should be considered a service organization with the dual purpose of assisting the centers and coordinating the study to meet its central objectives. There are problems inherent in this type of organization but a large scale cross-national study will have difficulty being completed without it.

Communication

In a study of this type the central office is the center of communication between the central office and either individual centers or all centers. At times individual centers contact other centers or wish to send out information or poll all of the other centers. Additionally there is a good deal of personal, yet research-related, correspondence.

With manuals and preliminary results and corrections of almost every item written, the amount of paper related to the study flying around the world can be tremendous. There seem to be two small procedures which help keep this correspondence orderly. First, each center should clearly mark all of its correspondence with its name and/or number, and date it. Second, the correspondence should refer plainly to the particular aspect of the study that is dealt with in each piece of correspondence. If the stages and various aspects of the study are outlined and numbered the correspondence can be more easily handled.

With all of the materials being circulated it becomes almost impossible to personally acknowledge every piece of correspondence. One of two approaches is suggested. Either a follow up system is used at each center asking for responses when one is not received from a first letter. Or one might enclose slips in all letters or bundles which ask the receiver to acknowledge receipt of the parcel and return the enclosed slip. International mails being what they are, one of these systems will assure that communication is in order.

Traveling Coordinator

The principal investigator for the overall study, one or more people from the central office, or people chosen from other centers should, if at all possible, visit all of the other stations periodically. When two people are conducting an experiment in a single room they usually find that they neglect to mention something to each other. They assume they do things the same way. One makes an important decision which seemed trivial at the time, and on and on. With participants scattered around the world, relying on mail for communication, there is no end to the items of information that may not be communicated, or may be miscommunicated or misinterpreted.

In one way or another visitations between stations should be conducted. The best situation would be to have one or two individuals who are intimately connected with one center spend some time at the central office getting an overall picture of where problems lie. Then they should go to each of the other centers, and they should have enough time there to really get into the procedures being used. They can make suggestions and point out how and where each center varies from the others. Not only might this help all of the centers on the same track, but the coordinators can keep complete records of their findings. At analysis time this information could be invaluable in explaining findings.

One side benefit of traveling coordinators is their possible morale effect. It often happens that following exact procedures outlined in a study's memoranda still leaves one with an uneasy feeling. Am I really doing this properly? Is this really the way we decided to do it?, and so on. The decisions that have to be made over the course of a study are so voluminous that one can have the feeling that he is doing things he did not agree to do. At that time bad feelings can develop either between centers or between some centers and the central office. A visit from the traveling coordinators at that time, or the knowledge that a visit is coming up, can ease many tensions. Interpersonal problems can be eased with personal explanations. The sense of detachment that can develop over time can be counteracted. Staff members who cannot attend conferences can get a better understanding of the project and a greater sense of involvement with whole from their meetings with the coordinator. Thus the reasons for including in the organization of the study at least one traveling coordinator are both practical and personal.

Conferences

By now it should be clear that communication and understanding between participants is crucial in cross-national studies. Many of the suggestions for organization given so far are geared toward facilitating this communication and understanding. However readings of the reports of a number of cross-national studies and our own experience clearly point to the value of face to face meetings periodically throughout the study.

"Joint development" may mean to some that an initial meeting at which the basic plan for the study is formulated constitutes sufficient meetings between the participants. In fact, at least three conferences are necessary in any cross-national study. The first conference sets the aims of the study and tentative procedures and schedule. The second conference follows the pilot testing phase and specifies final plans for data collection. The second conference employs the information gathered in the pilot tests to increase the reliability, validity, and, hence, value of the main study. The third conference comes after data collection and should deal with analysis and reporting. These seem to be the minimum number of conferences needed to successfully carry out a project of this kind. Often, however, many more are needed.

Conferences are expensive, but they are invaluable. If frequent contact is not possible in planning a cross-national study one might be better off retrenching and economizing in other ways.

Committees and Consultants

An economical and functional structure which has been used with good results in cross-national studies is a committee system. The study can be divided by areas of interest and instruments as well as steps in analysis. Committees of two or three or more participants, including staff members, can be help responsible for formulation of policy and reporting to all participants on these areas. Division of responsibility and distribution across centers maintains level of involvement, lessens bulk of correspondence, and increases quality of work because no one group or the central office is overloaded.

The committee system has another advantage of involving individuals in policy decisions. This decentralizing of responsibility benefits the project by inviting more and diverse (non-full professor) opinion. More members from each country directly add their knowledge of their country to the decisions which affect all countries. Additionally, being a members of a committee, which is essentially a recommending not a decision body, gives students a valuable educational experience.

In a large study there may well be specialists in all relevant

areas who are participants. However some funds for consult-
ants may be desirable. Methodology, statistical, sampling, linguistic and area or national specialists may be needed. In any
study problems arise that are not anticipated. In cross-national
studies problems arise that not only are not anticipated by the
researchers involved but are also new to the field. The answers
and technologies are not developed to the point where one can
feel totally confident that he can do it himself. We heartily
suggest preparing for and requesting specialized help when
needed.

Data Collection

The problems relating to data collection in cross-national research are of two types. The first type concerns the content and
meaning of instrument administration. The second deals with
the calendar data of the test administration relative to usual
and unusual events in the societies being studied.

The persons in each country who deal as data collectors with
the respondents, interact with the respondents in manners personally unique (varying according to the extent and quality of
their training) and socially appropriate (varying according to
cultural rigidity and knowledge of the tester-respondent roles).
The introduction, instructions, and instruments should be as
comparable as possible using all the precautions we have mentioned. Still, differences in presentation and associated rapport,
openness, and motivation can arise.

The initial question is: who administers the instruments?
Some uniformity across countries is necessary. The decision as
to who administers the tests must be made thoughtfully considering certainly age and sex, and possibly social class, professional role, and ethnicity.

Let us look at some possible examples of variability that
could arise due to different characteristics of the examiners.
In some countries there are far more coeducational schools
than in others. Will the faculties of these schools be all of the
same sex as the student body? Should the examiner be of the
same sex as the student body? Or if one is interviewing mothers, in some countries male interviewers would not be inappropriate whereas in other countries it would be rude to even suggest it. In a study dealing with lower-class subjects, University

people in some countries may not speak their language. Can and should peer interviewers or administrators be trained in all countries? Will gerontological subjects respond equivalently to University interviewers across countries?

The questions could go on indefinitely. The decision about who does the testing must be made according to the countries and subjects. And even then there may be gross differences in rapport btween test administrator or interviewer and respondent because of norms of openness and trust of strangers between countries and prevailing attitudes toward, experience with and knowledge of research and researchers. In any event the administrators themselves should be as uniform as possible.

Of course instructions should be standard. But in cross-national work it is especially necessary to decide whether the nation or subculture variables are made known to the subjects. Suppose a study were run today on stereotypes of European countries and political leaders, and the sample included the Common Market countries and Great Britain. If the study was presented as a public opinion study within each country one might expect a greater spread of opinion than if it was presented as a cross-national study. In the latter case individuals might be more prone to voicing stronger nationalistic sentiments than they might otherwise. The degree to which a person feels his responses represent him as an individual rather than as a representative of his country, social class, or subgroup can greatly influence the responses he gives. Additionally, the chauvinistic responses may be aroused by the motivational aspects of instructions, such that the subjects are differentially motivated to perform. For most purposes the introduction and instructions should be kept neutral as well as comparable.

The second set of cross-national problems of data collection relates to timing of administration. In most studies the data are best collected simultaneously in all countries. Obviously this is not always possible. The time element is a consideration in comparative analysis of all replication studies which can, after all, span long periods of time. Sometimes the design of a study makes it impossible to test in all areas at the same time. If one was investigating children's attitudes to their first day at school, test administration would have to be on or near that day. School starts each year at different times in different countries making it impossible to test at the same time in this example.

The time at which data are collected can conceivably influence results in indirect ways. Hudson *et al.* (undated mimeo paper, p. 4) reports:

> Although this consideration may not be critical for some problems, research has a way of yielding information on questions that might be anticipated. Therefore, even though the studies are focused upon issues that may represent relatively stable characteristics, not subject to change with fluctuations in local conditions, political, economic, etc., it may yield information upon some that are.

Particularly in research on children and adolescents, but also with adults, there may be changes, although temporary, over all subjects in a country on "stable characteristics" as the result of dramatic events such as national elections, assassinations, economic recession, or natural disasters. A spirited, well publicized election can raise doubts or hopes in children in one country whereas in another country no political activity warrants attitude change. World news may differentially affect people around the world as they view it in their perspective. Thus, the time of testing may carry varied meanings around the world because of differences in events and perspectives.

Analysis

Cross-national research has here been categorized as: 1) one-culture studies, in cultures other than that of the investigator; 2) two-culture comparative studies; 3) comparative studies in more than two cultures; and 4) replication studies which to date have been replications of the one-culture type study in yet another culture.

In one-culture studies analysis is aimed at describing the variables and/or relationships being investigated in that culture. In two-culture studies the goal of analysis is the description of the variables in both cultures and a comparison of how they are similar or different. Replication studies are analyzed for description and comparison as in the two-culture case, assuming that the replication of procedure is exact. If the replication is not exact, the comparative aspect of the study becomes more conjecture than statistical analysis. In all of these types of studies analysis is carried out under one or two investigators in one or two places. Although the analysis may be complex, communication among the people doing the analysis should not be complex.

Analysis of comparative studies in more than two cultures, and certainly in six and eight culture studies which are becoming more frequent, is extremely complex theoretically, statistically, and procedurally. The single most important procedural rule at this stage is that a central station must handle the analysis. Suggestions on hypotheses, treatments, and means of analysis can come from all participants in the study. The final decisions can be democratically made. But the actual statistical work should be done in one place so that all data, whether descriptive or comparative, are treated exactly alike. Additional analyses of portions of the data can be made within and between countries in any way the investigator (who may well be a graduate student) wishes. Nonetheless the primary data analysis for a more than two culture study must be done in one place under centralized control.

Were the analysis divided among the countries it would seem possible to specify exactly the statistical techniques and formulas to be used in each country. However it is also easy to see the multitude of ways in which the "same" work could be done. Studies of the magnitude of these cross-national studies are not feasibly analyzed except by computer. We are not to the point of having uniform programs for complex analysis. Therefore, by putting great care into deciding what techniques and which programs to use, and by running the data from all countries the same way in the same place, the final results are, if nothing else, uniform and comparable.

Reporting

Because we can envision no study giving the "final answer" to any question, we view all cross-national researches of any type as single units which may be added to the accumulation of social scientific knowledge. However, if answers are to be achieved from the universal human laboratory the results of cross-national research should be reported in such manner that the data from each unit of investigation, subculture and culture, as well as the comparative findings, are clear and complete enough to allow comparison with future studies testing the same and different hypotheses. This problem has caused grief and thought in relation to working with ethnographies and the Human Relations Area Files and considerable work has gone into procedures for making these data reliable enough for comparative analysis (Naroll 1962).

The day should come when the empirical data from cross-national studies are available in a centralized facility. If studies have been reported descriptively by culture and subculture and comparatively where proper, the centralized data will be very valuable.

Chapter 7

Perspective on Cross-National
Research in Social Science

WE HAVE REFERRED TO ONE ASPECT of research in Social
Science, cross-national social-psychological research, which we
see as becoming more discrete and identifiable. There exist, in
social science research, a number of research methods which
also investigate sociological, psychological, and cultural features of groups other than that of the investigator. In this
chapter we will expose the reader to some of these other methods and differentiate between them and cross-national social-
psychological research.

Cross-Cultural Research

Whiting (1954, p. 523), a leader in cross-cultural research,
states,

> The cross-cultural method utilizes data collected by anthro-
> pologists concerning the culture of various peoples through-
> out the world to test hypotheses concerning human behavior.
> Some of the hypotheses tested have been derived from theo-
> ries of cultural evolution, others from theories concerned
> with the integration of culture, and still others, particularly
> in recent years, from theories of individual and social psy-
> chology.

Recently, then, the aims of some cross-cultural studies have
been the same as the aims of cross-national social-psychologi-

cal studies. However, the methods, using data collected by anthropologists, are quite different, and the groups under study are different.

Anthropologists generally study people who live in close proximity to each other, who know each other, who constitute a group unto themselves, who have among them a discernible culture. In the past these societies have, for the most part, been small, isolated or semi-isolated, and primitive. Now and in the future increasing numbers of anthropologists will be working in urban areas in industrial societies. In the future, then, urban anthropologists and social psychologists working cross-nationally may sample from the same populations. But to date cross-national researchers and cross-cultural researchers have used different methods and samples to investigate what have for the most part been different types of problems. Therefore we suggest differentiating between these two types of research, bearing in mind that researchers in both fields can learn a great deal from the other.

Much of what we are calling cross-national is elsewhere called cross-cultural. A good example of this is LeVine's (1970) chapter called Cross-Cultural Study in Child Psychology. He restricts the chapter to quantitative studies which follow standard psychological practices and excludes anecdotal, ethnographic, and clinical studies. With Hess' chapter, in the same volume, on social class and ethnic variations in child development within Western societies, the full scope of what we are calling cross-national research is covered. We concur with LeVine's view "that intra-population and cross-population comparisons *should* be continuous and coordinated" and constitute a single area of study.

Anthropologists singly and in broad cross-cultural studies have dealt extensively with issues of importance in cross-national research, such as stimulus equivalence, language equivalence, and comparability of samples. Anthropologists have also become more sophisticated in the use of psychological instruments and have relied on psychological techniques with increasing frequency. As we dealt herein with the problems of method, design, and instrumentation, we drew on examples outside of accomplished social-psychological cross-national studies. We are well aware of the interdisciplinary approach mandatory to cross-national studies.

National Character Studies

National character studies, depending on the methods employed, resemble cross-national studies to varying degrees. They range from studies which are methodologically and theoretically quite different from cross-national studies to those which are identical except for a subtle theoretical difference.

A large portion of the "national character" literature is greatly dissimilar to cross-national research, being more anthropologically-oriented, culture-centered research which focuses on "learned cultural behavior" (Benedict 1934) and "systems of norms and values as evident in cultural goals and in the institutions and cultural products" (Duijker and Frijda 1960). This kind of "national character" studies must be noted here because they fit into the national character framework although they bear little resemblance to cross-national studies.

Another type of "national character" study differs from cross-national studies in intent. Its purpose is to describe and establish "the existence of 'national character' as a set of characteristics specific for a given nation as compared with others" (Duijker and Frijda 1960, p. 36). The goal of these "national character" studies is to describe the basic personality structure, the modal personality, or the pattern or patterns particular to, possibly peculiar to, a certain nation. "National character" studies may well be concerned with personality traits or patterns in the same way as cross-national studies. However these "national character" studies will *describe* the traits or patterns as representing predominant or unique factors common to the nation. Cross-national, social-psychological studies, on the other hand, will *compare* the traits and patterns of several countries in the light of their relation to subcultural and cultural influences.

A major difference between "national character" studies and cross-national studies lies in the relative emphasis on comparison of countries or cultures. The "national character" study is interested in comparison only as a means of highlighting the striking features of a particular society. The cross-national study has a central and dominant interest in systematic comparisons.

Cross-national studies investigate the relationships, the similarities and differences, among psychological variables within comparable sociological groups and situations across countries. Inferences are made from the collected data concerning psychological and behavioral functioning within and between the various samples in each country, and comparisons are made between the subsamples from all countries. The purpose of the cross-national investigation is to better understand these psychological functions in their sociological and cultural contexts.

Clearly, to describe *the* "national character" of a complex industrial nation is to gloss over the subcultural variations within the nation. For that reason Inkeles and Levinson (1954) suggest a "multimodal conception of national character." The multimodal conception "can accommodate the sub-cultural variations in socioeconomic class, geosocial region, ethnic group, and the like, which appear to exist in all modern nations" (p. 982). At this individual multimodal level of analysis the "national character" and cross-national research methods and conclusions are the most similar. The difference between the two types of research at this level is again a subtle difference in objectives. Inkeles and Levinson have suggested that "national character refers to relatively enduring personality characteristics and patterns that are modal (multimodal) among the adult members of the society" (p. 983). If the emphasis is placed on a description of the similarities and differences in the functional psychological relationships among the subgroups in a society it is a cross-national study.

Essentially we are saying that the cross-national objective of identifying similarities and differences in psychological functioning in the broadest sociological and cultural contexts may be enhanced by full descriptions of predominant patterns or "multimodal personalities" but by accentuating gross "modal personality" and cultural description the primary psychological objective is weakened.

Conclusions

This delineation of the relation between the various type of transcultural studies in the social sciences was intended to fortify the purpose of cross-national social psychological research. Berrien (1967, p. 34) concludes:

> To put the matter in extreme form, the psychologist is interested in the dynamic behavior rather than the artifacts of a

culture and from the character of this behavioral interplay, he wishes to infer something about the fundamental "subjective" basis for it. . . . As Campbell (1961) has congently pointed out, anthropological descriptions have provided the settings for the cross-cultural psychologist to test the generality of his otherwise culturally-bound theories.

Cross-national research allows us to test theories we believe true in our culture and to develop new theories from the variety of behaviors, personality, sociological and cultural variables found elsewhere. Utilizing techniques and instruments, as described in this book, future cross-national research will, we hope, bring us nearer to an understanding of what makes men similar and what makes men different around the world.

References

Ach, N. (1964), "Determining Tendencies," in J. M. Mandler and G. Mandler, eds. *Thinking: from Association to Gestalt.* New York: Wiley, 201–207.

Adorno, T. W., Frenkel-Brunswik, E., Levinson, D. J., and Sanford, R. N. (1950), *The Authoritarian Personality.* New York: Harper.

Allport, G. W. and Odbert, H. S. (1936), "Trait-Names: a Psycho-Lexical Study," *Psychological Monographs,* 47 (1, Whole No. 211).

Allport, G. W., and Pettigrew, T. F. (1957), "Cultural Influence on the Perception of Movement: the Trapezoidal Illusion among Zulus," *Journal of Abnormal and Social Psychology,* 55, 104–113.

Allport, G. W., Vernon, P. E., and Lindzey, G. (1960) *Manual, Study of Values,* 3rd ed., Boston: Houghton-Mifflin.

Anderson, H. H., and Anderson, G. L. (1961), "Image of the Teacher by Adolescent Children in Seven Countries," *American Journal of Orthopsychiatry,* 31, 481–492.

Anderson, N. H. (1968), "Likableness Ratings of 555 Personality-Trait Words," *Journal of Personality and Social Psychology,* 9, 272–279.

Angelini, A. L. (1955), "Un Novo Metodo para Avaliar a Motivação Humana." Unpublished doctoral dissertation, Brazil: Universidade de Sao Paulo.

Angelini, A. L. (1966), "Measuring the Achievement Motive in Brazil," *Journal of Social Psychology,* 68, 35–40.

Atkinson, J. W., ed. (1958), *Motives in Fantasy, Action, and Society.* Princeton: Van Nostrand.

Bass, B. M. (1955), "Authoritarianism or Acquiescence?" *Journal of Abnormal Social Psychology,* 51, 616–623.

Bavelas, A. (1942), "A Method of Investigating Individual and Group Ideology," *Sociometry,* 5, 371–377.

Benedict, R. F. (1934), *Patterns of Culture*. Boston: Houghton-Mifflin.

Bengtson, V. L. (1969), "Differences between Subsamples in Level of Present Role Activity," Ch. 3 in *Adjustment to Retirement*, R. J. Havighurst *et al.*, eds. New York: Humanities Press.

Berrien, F. K. (1967), "Methodological and Related Problems in Cross-Cultural Research," *International Journal of Psychology*, Vol. 2, No. 1, 33–43.

Biesheuvel, S. (1958), "Methodology in the Study of Attitudes of Africans," *Journal of Social Psychology*, 47, 169–184.

Birney, R. C. (1958), "Thematic Content and the Cue Characteristics of Pictures," in *Motives in Fantasy, Action, and Society*, J. W. Atkinson, ed. Princeton: Van Nostrand, 630–643.

Bleuler, M. and Bleuler, R. (1935), "Rorschach's Ink-blot Test and Racial Psychology: Mental Peculiarities of Moroccans," *Character and Personality*, 4, 97–114.

Bogardus, E. S. (1925), "Measuring Social Distances," *Journal of Applied Sociology*, 9, 299–308.

Bogardus, E. S. (1928), *Immigration and Race Attitudes*. Boston: D. C. Heath and Co.

Brodman, K., Erdmann, A. J., Jr., Lorge, I. Wolff, H. G., Broadbent, T. H. (1951), "The Cornell Medical Index," *Journal of the American Medical Association*, 145, 152–157.

Brodman, K., Erdmann, A. J., Jr., and Wolff, H. G. (1956), *Cornell Medical Index Questionnaire Manual*. (Rev. 1956). New York City: Cornell University Medical School.

Brown, R. (1965), *Social Psychology*. New York: The Free Press.

Butt, D. S. and Signori, E. I. (1965), "Personality Factors of a Canadian Sample of Male University Students," *Psychological Reports*, 16, 1117–1121.

Campbell, D. T. (1952), "The Bogardus Social Distance Scale," *Sociology and Social Research*, 36, 322–326.

Campbell, D. T. and Fiske, D. W. (1959), "Convergent and Discriminant Validation by the Multitrait-Multimethod Matrix," *Psychological Bulletin*, 56, No. 2, March, 81–95.

Campbell, D. T. (1961), "The Mutual Methodological Relevance of Anthropology and Psychology," *Psychological An-*

thropology, L. K. Hsu, ed. Homewood, Ill.: Dorsey Press, 333–352.

Campbell, D. T. and LeVine, R. A. (March 1965), "Propositions about Ethnocentrism from Social Science Theories," mimeo, working draft.

Carr, A. C., Forer, B. R., Henry, W. E., Piotrowski, Z. A. (1960), *The Prediction of Overt Behavior through the Use of Projective Techniques*. Chapter by Bertram R. Forer, pp. 6–17. Springfield, Ill. Charles C. Thomas.

Cattell, R. B. (1957), *Personality and Motivation Structure and Measurement*. New York: World Book.

Cattell, R. B., ed. (1959–63), *Handbooks to the Children's, High School and Adults' (16PF) Questionnaires*, Institute of Personality and Ability Testing. Champaign, Illinois.

Caudill, W. (1952), "Japanese-American Personality and Acculturation," *Genetic Psychology Monographs*, **45**, Feb., 5–101.

Chance, N. A. (1962), "Conceptual and Methodological Problems in Cross-Cultural Health Research," *American Journal of Public Health*, **52**, 410–417.

Christie, R. (1954), "Authoritarianism Re-examined," in R. Christie and Marie Jahoda, eds., *Studies in the Scope and Method of "The Authoritarian Personality."* New York: Free Press.

Christie, R. (1956), "Eysenck's Treatment of the Personality of Communists," *Psychological Bulletin*, **53**, 411–430.

Christie, R., Havel, J. and Seidenberg, B. (1958), "Is the F Scale Irreversible?" *Journal of Abnormal and Social Psychology*, **56**, 143–159.

Coelho, G. B., Silber, E., and Hamburg, D. A. (1962), "Use of the Student-TAT to Assess Coping Behavior in Hospitalized, Normal, and Exceptionally Competent College Freshmen," *Perceptual and Motor Skills*, **14**, 355–365.

Cohn, T. S. (1953), "The Relation of the F Scale to a Response to Answer Positively," *American Psychologist*, **8**, 335. (Abstract).

Coladarci, A. (1959), "The Measurement of Authoritarianism in Japanese Educators," *California Journal of Educational Research*, **10**, 137–141.

Coleman, J. (1969), "The Methods of Sociology" in *A Design for*

Sociology, R. Bierstedt, ed. Monograph #9, American Academy of Political and Social Science, April, 1961.

Couch, A. & Keniston, K. (1960), "Yeasayers and Naysayers: Agreeing Response Set as a Personality Variable," *Journal of Abnormal Social Psychology*, **60**, 151–174.

Coulter, T. (1953), "An Experimental and Statistical Study of the Relationship of Prejudice and Certain Personality Variables." Unpublished doctoral dissertation. University of London.

Cronbach, L. J. (1949), *Essentials of Psychological Testing*. New York: Harper.

Cronbach, L. J. (1960), *Essentials of Psychological Testing*, 2nd ed., New York: Harper and Row.

Dember, W. N. (1965), "The New Look in Motivation," *American Scientist*, **53**, 409–427.

Dennis, W. (1942), "The Performance of Hopi Children on the Goodenough Draw-a-Man Test." *Journal of Comparative Psychology* **34**: 341–348.

Dennis, W. (1943), "Animism and Related Tendencies in Hopi Children," *Journal of Abnormal and Social Psychology*, **38**, 21–36.

Dennis, W. (1951), "Cultural and Developmental Factors in Perception," in *An Approach to Personality*, R. R. Blake and G. V. Ramsey, eds. New York: Ronald Press.

Dennis, W. (1953), "Animistic Thinking Among College and University Students," *Scientific Monthly*, **76**, 247–249.

Dennis, W. (1957a), "A Cross-Cultural Study of the Reinforcement of Child Behavior," *Child Development*, Vol. 28, No. 4, 431–438.

Dennis, W. (1957b), "Uses of Common Objects as Indicators of Cultural Orientation," *Journal of Abnormal Social Psychology*, **55**, 21–28.

Dennis, W. (1966a), "Goodenough Scores, Art Experience, and Modernization," *Journal of Social Psychology*, **68**, 211–228.

Dennis, W. (1966b), *Group Values through Children's Drawings*. New York: John Wiley & Sons.

Dennis, W., and Russell, R. W. (1940), "Piaget's Questions Applied to Zuni Children," *Child Development*, **11**, 181–187.

Dennis, W., and Uras, A. (1965), "The Religious Content of Human Figure Drawings Made by Nuns," *Journal of Psychology,* **61,** 263–266.

Devereux, E. C., Jr., Bronfenbrenner, U., and Suci, G. J. (1962), "Patterns of Parent Behavior in the United States of America and the Federal Republic of Germany: A Cross-National Comparison," *International Social Science Journal,* Vol. 14, No. 3.

DeVos, G. (1952), "A Quantitative Approach to Affective Symbolism in Rorschach Responses," *Journal of Projective Techniques,* **16,** 133–150.

DeVos, G. (1954), "A Comparison of Personality Differences in Two Generations of Japanese Americans by Means of the Rorschach Test," *Nagoya Journal of Medical Science,* **17,** 153–265.

DeVos, G. (1955), "A Quantitative Rorschach Assessment of Maladjustment and Rigidity in Acculturating Japanese-Americans," *Genetic Psychology Monographs,* **52,** 51–87.

DeVos, G. (1961), "Symbolic Analysis in the Cross-Cultural Study of Personality," in *Studying Personality Cross-Culturally,* Bert Kaplan, ed. Evanston, Ill.: Row, Peterson, 599–635.

DeVos, G. (1966), "Transcultural Diagnosis of Mental Health by Means of Psychological Tests." University of California: Berkeley, Institute of Human Development. Working Paper.

DeVos, G. (1969), "Cultural Psychology: Comparative Studies of Human Behavior," in *Handbook of Social Psychology,* Vol. IV, Lindzey and Aronson, eds. Reading, Mass.: Addison-Wesley.

Dorr, M. (1951), "Age, Sex, and Social Status Differences in Children's Verbally Expressed Values." Unpublished Ph.D. dissertation, Department of Education, University of Chicago.

Dreyer, P. H. (1970), "The Meaning and Validity of the 'Phenomenal Self' for American Indian Students." National Study of American Indian Education. *Final Report.* Series III, No. 7.

DuBois, G. (1944), *People of Alor.* Minneapolis: University of Minnesota Press.

Duijker, H. C. J., and Frijda, N. H. (1960), *National Character and National Stereotype: Methods in National Character Study*. Amsterdam: North Holland Publishing Company.

Edwards, A. (1954), *Statistical Methods for the Behavioral Sciences*. New York: Rinehart.

Edwards, A. L. (1957a), *The Social Desirability Variable in Personality Assessment and Research*. New York: Dryden Press.

Edwards, A. L. (1957b), *Techniques of Attitude Scale Construction*. New York: Appleton-Century.

Ervin, S. M. (1964), "Language and TAT Content in Bilinguals," *Journal of Abnormal and Social Psychology*, **68**, 500–507.

Eysenck, H. J. (1954), *The Psychology of Politics*. London: Routledge and Kegan Paul.

Field, P. B., Maldonado-Sierra, E. D., and Coelho, G. V. (1963), "A Student-TAT Measure of Competence: A Cross-Cultural Replication in Puerto Rico," *Perceptual and Motor Skills*, **16**, 195–198.

Flanagan, J. C. (1954), "The Critical Incident Technique," *Psychological Bulletin*, **51**, 327–358.

Forer, B. R. (1960), "Sentence Completion," in *The Prediction of Overt Behavior through the Use of Projective Techniques*, A. C. Carr *et al.*, eds. Springfield, Ill.: C. C. Thomas.

Frank, L. K. (1939), "Projective Methods for the Study of Personality," *Journal of Psychology*, **8**, 389–413.

Froelich, W. D.; Becker, J.; Bengtson, V. L.; and Bigot, A. (1969) "The Problem of Cross-national Reliability of Ratings; Some Tentative Approaches and Findings." Ch. 2 in *Adjustment to Retirement*, edited by Havighurst, Munnichs, Neugarten and Thomae. New York: Humanities Press, 1969. Assen, Netherlands: Van-Gorcum, 1969.

Germani, G. (1960), *Occupational Categories*. Working Papers of the Institute of Sociology. No. 25, University of Buenos Aires, Department of Sociology.

Gillespie, J. M. and Allport, G. W. (1955), *Youth's Outlook on the Future; A Cross-National Study*. Garden City, New York: Doubleday.

Goodenough, F. L. (1926), *Measurement of Intelligence by Drawings*. New York: World Book.

Gough, H. G. (1960), "Cross-Cultural Studies of the Socialization Continuum," *American Psychologist*, 15, 410–411.

Gough, H. G. (1965), "Cross-Cultural Validity of a Measure of Asocial Behavior," *Psychological Reports*, 17, 379–387.

Gough, H. G. and Chun, K. (1968), "Validation of the CPI Femininity Scale," *Psychological Reports*, 22, 155–160.

Gough, H. G. and DeVos, G. (1968), "Japanese Validation of the CPI Social Maturity Index," *Psychological Reports*, 22, 143–146.

Gough, H. G. and Sandhu, H. S. (1964), "Validity of the CPI Socialization Scale in India," *Journal of Abnormal and Social Psychology*, 68, 544–547.

Green, B. F. (1954), "Attitude Measurement," in *Handbook of Social Psychology. Vol. 1 Theory and Method*, G. Lindzey, ed. Cambridge, Mass.: Addison-Wesley.

Grinder, R. and McMichael, R. (1963), "Cultural Influences on Conscience Development: Resistance to Temptation and Guilt among Samoans and American Caucasians," *Journal of Abnormal and Social Psychology*, 66, 503–507.

Guilford, J. P. (1954), *Psychometric Methods*. 2nd ed. New York: McGraw-Hill.

Gutmann, D. (1964), "An Exploration of Ego Configurations in Middle and Later Life," in *Personality in Middle and Latter Life*, Bernice L. Neugarten, ed. New York: Prentice-Hall.

Gutmann, D. (1966), "Mayan Aging—A Comparative TAT Study," *Psychiatry*, 29, 246–259.

Gutmann, D. (1969), "Psychological Naturalism in Cross-Cultural Studies," in *Naturalistic Viewpoints in Psychological Research*, Edwin P. Willems and Harold L. Raush, eds. New York: Holt, Rinehart & Winston, 162–176.

Hallowell, A. I. (1955), "The Rorschach Test in Personality and Culture Studies," in his *Culture and Experience*. Philadelphia: University of Pennsylvania Press, 32–74.

Hammer, E. F. (1965), "Critique of Swensen's Empirical Evaluations of Human Figure Drawings," in *Handbook of*

Projective Techniques, Bernard I. Murstein, ed. New York: Basic Books, 655–659.

Hammer, E. F. (1968), "Projective Drawings," in *Projective Techniques in Personality Assessment,* A. I. Rabin, ed. New York: Springer, 366–396.

Harbison, F., and Myers, C. A. (1964), *Education, Manpower and Economic Growth; Strategies of Human Resource Development.* New York: McGraw-Hill.

Harris, D. B. (1961), *Measuring the Psychological Maturity of Children: A Revision and Extension of the Good-enough Draw-a-Man Test.* Tarrytown-on-Hudson, N. Y.: World Book Company.

Havighurst, R. J. (1954), *Studies of Children and Society in New Zealand.* Christchurch, New Zealand: Canterbury University Department of Education (Mimeographed).

Havighurst, R. J. (1957a), "The Leisure Activities of the Middle-Aged," *American Journal of Sociology,* **43,** 152–162.

Havighurst, R. J. (1957b), "The Social Competence of Middle-Aged People," *Genetic Psychology Monographs,* **56,** 297–375.

Havighurst, R. J. (1969), "Measuring Socio-economic Status in the Cross-National Study of Children and Adolescents," unpublished working paper.

Havighurst, R. J. (1970a) "The Reliability of Rating Scales Used in Analyzing Interviews with Parents, Students, Teachers, and Community Leaders." National Study of American Indian Education. *Final Report.* Series IV. No. 9.

Havighurst, R. J. (1970b), "The Sample Used in the Research." in *Technical Report,* Vol. 1 "Coping Style and Achievement: A Cross-National Study of Children."

Havighurst, R. J., Dubois, M. E., Csikszentmihalyi, M., and Doll, R. (1965), *A Cross-National Study of Buenos Aires and Chicago Adolescents.* Basel: S. Karger.

Havighurst, R. J., and Gouveia, A. J. (1969), *Brazilian Secondary Education and Socioeconomic Development.* New York: Praeger.

Havighurst, R. J., Gunther, M. K., and Pratt, I. E. (1946), "Environment and the Draw-a-Man Test," *Journal of Abnormal and Social Psychology,* **41,** 50–63.

Havighurst, R. J., and Hilkevitch, R. R. (1944), "The Intelligence of Indian Children as Measured by a Performance Scale," *Journal of Abnormal and Social Psychology*, **39**, 419–433.

Havighurst, R. J., and MacDonald, D. V. (1955), "Development of the Ideal Self in New Zealand and American Children," *Journal of Educational Research*, **49**, 269–273.

Havighurst, R. J., and Moreira, J. R. (1965), *Society and Education in Brazil*. Pittsburgh: University of Pittsburgh Press.

Havighurst, R. J., Munnichs, J., Neugarten, B. L., and Thomae, Hans (1969), *Adjustment to Retirement; A Cross-National Pilot Study*. New York: Humanities Press.

Havighurst, R. J., and Neugarten, B. L. (1955), *American Indian and White Children*. Chicago: University of Chicago Press.

Havighurst, R. J., Robinson, Z., and Dorr, M. (1946), "The Development of the Ideal Self in Childhood and Adolescence," *Journal of Educational Research*, **40**, 241–257.

Heise, D. R. (1969), "Some Methodological Issues in Semantic Differential Research," *Psychological Bulletin*, **72**, 406–422.

Helm, J., DeVos, G., and Carterette, T. (1963), "Variations in Personality and Ego Identification within a Slave Indian Kin-community," *Contributions to Anthropology, 1960*. National Museum of Canada. Bulletin 190, Part 2.

Henry, W. E. (1947), "The TAT in the Study of Culture-Personality Relations," *Genetic Psychology Monographs*, **35**, Feb., 7–135.

Henry, W. E. (1960), in *Handbook of Research Methods in Child Development*, Paul H. Mussen, ed. New York: Wiley.

Hodge, R. W., Treiman, R. J., and Rossi, P. H. (1966), "A Comparative Study of Occupational Prestige," in *Class, Status and Power: Social Stratification in Comparative Perspective*, Reinhard Bendix and Seymour Martin Lipset, eds., 2nd ed. New York: Free Press, 309–321.

Hollen, C. C. (1967), "The Stability of Values and Value Systems." Unpublished M.A. thesis, Michigan State University Library.

Holtzman, W. H. (1965), "Cross-Cultural Research on Personality Development," *Human Development,* **8**, 65–86.

Holtzman, W. H. (1968), "Holtzman Inkblot Technique," in *Projective Techniques,* A. I. Rabin, ed. New York: Springer, 136–171.

Holtzman, W. H., Diaz-Guerrero, R., Swartz, J. D., and Tapia, Luis Lara (1968), "Cross-Cultural Longitudinal Research on Child Development: Studies of American and Mexican Schoolchildren," in *Minnesota Symposium on Child Psychology.* Vol. II, J. P. Hill, ed. Minneapolis: University of Minnesota Press.

Holtzman, W. H., Thorpe, J. S., Swartz, J. D., and Herron, E. W. (1961), *Inkblot Perception and Personality.* Austin, Texas: University of Texas Press.

Horton, D. L., Marlowe, D., and Crowne, D. P. (1963), "The Effect of Instructional Set and Need for Social Approval on Commonality of Word Association Responses," *Journal of Abnormal Social Psychology,* **66**, 67–72.

Hudson, B. B., Barakat, M. K., and La Forge, R., "Problems and Methods of Cross-Cultural Research," undated mimeo paper.

Hudson, W. (1960), "Pictorial Depth Perception in Sub-cultural Groups in Africa," *The Journal of Social Psychology,* **52**, 183–208.

Hutchinson, B. (1960), *Mobilidade e Trabalho.* Rio de Janeiro: Centro Brasileiro de Pesquisas Educacionais.

Inkeles, A., and Levinson, D. J. (1954), "National Character: The Study of Modal Personality and Socio-cultural Systems," *Handbook of Social Psychology.* Vol. II, G. Lindzey, ed. Cambridge, Mass.: Addison-Wesley, 977–1020.

Jahoda, G. (1958), "Child Animism: I. A Critical Survey of Cross-Cultural Research," *Journal of Social Psychology,* **47**, 197–212.

Jahoda, G. (1958), "Child Animism: II. A Study in West Africa," *Journal of Social Psychology,* **47**, 213–222.

Jahoda, G. (1958), "Immanent Justice Among West African Children," *Journal of Social Psychology,* **47**, 241–248.

Jakobovits, L. A. (1966), "Comparative Psycholinguistics in the

Study of Cultures," *International Journal of Psychology*, **1**, 15–37.

Kahl, J. A. (1962), "Urbanizacao e Mudancao Ocupacionais no Brasil," *America Latina*, **5**, 21–30.

Kahl, J. A. (1968), *The Measurement of Modernism: A Study of Values in Brazil and Mexico*. Austin, Texas: The University of Texas Press.

Karon, B. P. (1968), "Problems of Validities," in *Projective Techniques in Personality Assessment*, A. I. Robin, ed. New York: Springer, 102.

Kendall, M. G. (1955), *Rank Correlation Methods*. London: Griffin.

Kennedy, W. A., and Lindner, R. S. (1964), "A Normative Study of the Goodenough Draw-a-Man Test on Southeastern Negro Elementary School Children," *Child Development*, **34**, 33–62.

Kent, G. H., and Rosanoff, A. J. (1910), "A Study of Association in Insanity," *American Journal of Insanity*, **67**, 37–96.

Khatena, J. (1964), "Comparative Performance on the CPM and DAM in Two Singapore Schools." Unpublished M. A. thesis, University of Singapore.

Kinsey, A. C., Pomeroy, W. B., Martin, C. E., and Gebhard, P. H. (1948, 1953) *Sexual Behavior in the Human Male. Sexual Behavior in the Human Female*. Philadelphia: Saunders.

Kogan, Nathan and Wallach, Michael A. (1964), *Risk-Taking: A Study in Cognition and Personality*. New York: Holt, Rinehart & Winston.

Knudsen, A. K., Gorham, D. R., and Moseley, E. C. (1966), "Universal Popular Responses to Inkblots in Five Cultures: Denmark, Germany, Hong Kong, Mexico, and United States," *Journal of Projective Techniques and Personality Assessment*, **30**, 135–142.

Kroeber, T. C. (1964), "The Coping Functions of the Ego Mechanisms," in *The Study of Lives*, R. W. White, ed. New York: Atherton, 178–199.

Kubo, Shunichi (1969), "On the Difficulties of Japanese Translation of the Instruments Used for International Researches." Unpublished working paper.

Lansky, L. M. (1968), "Story Completion Methods," in *Projective Techniques in Personality Assessment*, A. I. Rabin, ed. New York: Springer, 290–327.

Lavin, D. E. (1965), *The Prediction of Academic Performance.* New York: Russell Sage Foundation.

Leighton, D. C., and Kluckhohn, C. (1947), *Children of the People.* Cambridge, Mass.: Harvard University Press.

Lerner, E. (1937), *Constraint Areas and the Moral Judgment of Children.* Menasha, Wisconsin: Banta.

Levensky, K. (1970) "The Performance of American Indian Children on the Draw-a-Man Test." National Study of American Indian Education. *Final Report.* Series III. No. 2.

LeVine, R. A. (1966), *Dreams and Deeds: Achievement Motivation in Nigeria.* Chicago: University of Chicago Press.

Levine, R. A. (1970), "Cross-Cultural Study in Child Psychology," in *Carmichael's Manual of Child Psychology,* Paul Mussen, ed. New York: Wiley.

Lindzey, G. (1961), *Projective Techniques and Cross-Cultural Research.* New York: Appleton-Century-Crofts.

Liu, P. Y., and Meredith, G. M. (1966), "Personality Structure of Chinese College Students in Taiwan and Hong Kong," *The Journal of Social Psychology,* **70,** 165–166.

Lucas, C. M., and Horrocks, J. E. (1960), "An Experimental Approach to the Analysis of Adolescent Needs," *Child Development,* **31,** 479–487.

Machover, K. (1949), *Personality Projection in the Drawing of the Human Figure.* Springfield, Ill.: Charles C. Thomas.

Manaster, G. J. (1969a), "Coping Styles, Sense of Competence and Achievement." Unpublished dissertation, University of Chicago.

Manaster, G. J. (1969b), "Modernism and Risk-Taking of Puerto Rican Adolescents." Paper presented at the Interamerican Psychological Congress, Montevideo, Uraguay.

Manaster, G. J. (1970), "Social Attitudes Inventory," in *Coping Styles and Achievement: A Cross-National Study of Children,* Report Vol. I, R. Peck, R. Havighurst, and K. Miller, eds. University of Texas.

McClelland, D. C., ed. (1955), *Studies in Motivation.* New York: Appleton-Century-Crofts.

McClelland, D. C. (1961), *The Achieving Society.* Princeton: Van Nostrand.

McClelland, D., Atkinson, J. W., Clark, R. A., and Lowell, E. L.

(1953), *The Achievement Motive*. New York: Appleton-Century.

Meade, R. D., Whittaker, J. O. (1967), A Cross-Cultural Study of Authoritarianism," *Journal of Social Psychology*, **72**, 3–7.

Melikian, L. (1959), "Authoritarianism and Its Correlates in Egyptian Culture and in the United States," *Journal of Social Issues*, **15**, 58–68.

Melvin, D. (1955), "An Experimental and Statistical Study of Two Primary Social Attitudes." Unpublished doctoral dissertation, University of London.

Meredith, G. M. (1966), "Amae and Acculturation Among Japanese-American College Students in Hawaii," *The Journal of Social Psychology*, **70**, 171–180.

Messick, S. J., and Jackson, D. N. (1957), "Authoritarianism or Acquiescence in Bass' Data," *Journal of Abnormal Social Psychology*, **54**, 424–425.

Michelis, E. (1969), "Development of an Objective Coding System." Paper read at the AERA meeting, Los Angeles, California .

Moran, L. J. (1966), "Generality of Word-Association Response Sets," *Psychological Monographs*, **80**, 2 (Whole No. 612).

Moran, L. J., Mefferd, R. B., and Kimble, J. P. (1964), "Idiodynamic Sets in Word Association," *Psychological Monographs*, **78**, (Whole No. 579).

Moran, L. J., and Murakawa, M. (1968), "Japanese and American Association Structures," *Journal of Verbal Learning and Verbal Behavior*, **7**, 176–181.

Morgan, C. D., and Murray, H. A. (1935), "A Method for Investigating Fantasies: The Thematic Apperception Test," *Archives of Neurological Psychiatry*, **34**, 289–306.

Murstein, B. I. (1965), "Reliability," in *Handbook of Projective Techniques*, Bernard I. Murstein, ed. New York: Basic Books.

Naroll, R. (1962), *Data Quality Control—A New Research Technique*. New York: Free Press of Glencoe.

Neuringer, C. (1968), "A Variety of Thematic Methods," in *Projective Techniques in Personality Assessment*, A. I. Rabin, ed. New York: Springer, 222–261.

Nobechi, M. and Kimura, T. (1957), "Study of Values Applied to Japanese Students," *Psychologia*, 1, 120–122.

Nunnally, J. C. (1967), *Psychometric Theory*, New York: Mc-Graw-Hill.

Organization for Comparative Social Research (1954), *Journal of Social Issues*, Vol. X, No. 4.

Osgood, C. E. (1960), "The Cross-Cultural Generality of Visual-Verbal Synesthetic Tendencies," *Behavioral Science*, Vol. 5, No. 2, 146–169.

Osgood, C. E. (1962), "Studies in the Generality of Affective Meaning Systems," *American Psychologist*, **17**, 10–28.

Osgood, C. E. (1964), "Semantic Differential Technique in the Comparative Study of Cultures," *American Anthropologist*, **66**, 171–200.

Osgood, C. E., Suci, G. J., and Tannenbaum, P. H. (1957), *The Measurement of Meaning*. Urbana, Ill.: University of Illinois Press.

Peabody, D. (1961), "Attitude Content and Agreement Set in Scales of Authoritarianism, Dogmatism, Anti-Semitism, and Economic Conservatism," *Journal of Abnormal and Social Psychology*, **63**, 1–11.

Peabody, D. (1966), "Authoritarian Scales and Response Bias," *Psychological Bulletin*, **65**, 11–23.

Peck, R., and Diaz-Guerrero, R. (1963), "Two Core-Culture Patterns and the Diffusion of Values Across Their Border," in *Proceedings of the Seventh Inter-American Congress of Psychology*. Mexico City: Sociedad Interamericana de Psicologia.

Peck, R., Havighurst, R., Miller, K., eds. (1970), *Coping Styles and Achievement: A Cross-National Study of Children*, Technical Report, Vol. I, The University of Texas at Austin.

Penner, L., Homant, R., and Rokeach, M. (1968), "Comparison of Rank-Order and Paired-Comparison Methods for Measuring Value Systems," *Perceptual and Motor Skills*, **27**, 417–418.

Piaget, J. (1930), *The Child's Conception of the World*. New York: Harcourt, Brace.

Piaget, J. (1932), *The Moral Judgment of the Child*. New York: Harcourt, Brace.

Piaget, J. (1947), "The Moral Development of the Adolescent in

Two Types of Society, Primitive and Modern." Lecture given July 24, 1947 at the UNESCO Seminar on Education for International Understanding, Paris (mimeographed).

Prothro, E., and Melikian, L. (1953), "The California Public Opinion Scale in an Authoritarian Culture," *Public Opinion Quarterly*, **17**, 353–362.

Rabin, A. I., and Limuaco, J. A. (1959), "Sexual Differentiation of American and Filipino Children as Reflected in the Draw-A-Person Test," *Journal of Social Psychology*, **50**, 207–211.

Rivers, W. H. R. (1901), "Cambridge Anthropological Expedition to Torres Straits," *Report, Vol. II, Pt. L: Introduction and Vision*. Cambridge, England: Cambridge University Press.

Rokeach, M. (1960), *The Open and Closed Mind*. New York: Basic Books.

Rokeach, M. (1968a), *Beliefs, Attitudes and Values*. San Francisco: Jossey-Bass.

Rokeach, M. (1968b), "A Theory of Organization and Change within Value-Attitude Systems," *Journal of Social Issues*, **24**, 13–33.

Rokeach, Milton (1968–69), "The Role of Values in Public Opinion Research," *The Public Opinion Quarterly*, **32**, 547–559.

Rokeach, Milton (1969), "The Measurement of Values and Value Systems." Prepublication copy, mimeo.

Rosen, B. C. (1962), "Socialization and Achievement Motivation in Brazil," *American Sociological Review*, Vol. 27, No. 5, 612–624.

Rosen, B. C. (1964), "The Achievement Syndrome and Economic Growth in Brazil," *Social Forces*, Vol. 42, No. 3, 341–354.

Rosenwald, G. C. (1968), "The Thematic Apperception Test (TAT)," in *Projective Techniques in Personality Assessment*, A. I. Rabin, ed. New York: Springer, 172–221.

Rosenzweig, M. R. (1961), "Comparisons among Word-Association Responses in English, French, German, and Italian," *The American Journal of Psychology*, Vol. 74, No. 3, 347–360.

Russell, R. W. (1940), "Studies in Animism, II. The Development of Animism," *Journal of Genetic Psychology*, 56, 353–366.

Russell, W. A., and Jenkins, J. J. (1954), "The Complete Minnesota Norms for Responses to 100 Words from the Kent-Rosanoff Word Association Test." Technical Report N. 11, University of Minnesota, Contract N8 ONR 66216, Office of Naval Research.

Schaw, L. C., and Henry, W. E. (1956), "A Method for the Comparison of Groups: A Study in Thematic Apperception," *Genetic Psychology Monographs*, **54**, 207–253.

Scheier, I. H., and Cattell, R. B. (1963), "The IPAT Anxiety Scale," Champaign, Ill.: Institute of Personality and Ability Testing.

Schneider, C. J., and Streib, G. F. (1969), "Self-Perception of Health in Longitudinal Perspective." Abstract appearing in the Program of the 8th International Congress of Gerontology. Washington, D. C.

Segall, M. H., Campbell, D. T., and Herskovits, M. J. (1963), "Cultural Differences in the Perception of Geometric Illusions," *Science*, Vol. 139, No. 3556, 769–771.

Segall, M. H., Campbell, D. T., and Herskovits, M. J. (1966), *The Influence of Culture on Visual Perception.* Indianapolis: Bobbs Merrill.

Shanas, E., Townsend, P., Wedderburn, D., Friis, H., Milhoj, P., and Stehouwer, J. (1968), *Old People in Three Industrial Societies.* New York: Atherton Press.

Smith, D. H., and Inkeles, A. (1966), "The O-M Scale: A Comparative Socio-psychological Measure of Individual Modernity," *Sociometry*, **29**, 353–377.

Spranger, E. *Types of Men,* Translated from 5th German edition of *Lebensformen* by Carl J. W. Pigors, Halle: Max Niemeyer Verlag.

Swartz, J., and Holtzman, W. H. (1963), "Group Method of Administration for the Holtzman Inkblot Technique," *Journal of Clinical Psychology*, **19**, 433–453.

Swensen, C. (1955), "Sexual Differentiation on the Draw-A-Person," *Journal of Clinical Psychology*, **11**, 37–41.

Swensen, C. H. Jr. (1965), "The Draw-A-Person Test," in *Handbook of Projective Techniques*, Bernard I. Murstein, ed. New York: Basic Books, 609–654.

Thurstone, L. L. (1937), *The Reliability and Validity of Tests.* Ann Arbor: Edwards.

Triandis, H. C., and Triandis, L. M. (1960), "Race, Social Class, Religion, and Nationality as Determinants of Social Distance," *Journal of Abnormal and Social Psychology,* Vol. 61, No. 1, 110–118.

Triandis, H. C., and Triandis, L. M. (1962), "A Cross-Cultural Study of Social Distance," *Psychological Monographs,* Vol. 76, No. 21, Whole No. 540.

Tsujioka, B., and Cattell, R. B. (1965), "A Cross-Cultural Comparison of Second-Stratum Questionnaire Personality Factor Structures—Anxiety and Extraversion, in America and Japan," *The Journal of Social Psychology,* **65,** 205–219.

United States Office of Education, *Authority, Rules and Aggression: A Cross National Study of Socialization into Compliance Systems.* Project No. 2947, Field Manual by June L. Tapp. Washington, D. C.: U. S. Government Printing Office.

United States Office of Education, Bureau of Research, *International Project for the Evaluation of Educational Achievement.* Final Report, Project No. 6–2527. Washington, D. C.: U. S. Government Printing Office.

Warner, W. L., Meeker, M. L., and Eells, K. (1960), *Social Class in America.* New York: Harper Torchbooks.

White, R. W., ed. (1964), *The Study of Lives: Essays on Personality in Honor of Henry A. Murray.* New York: Atherton.

Whiting, J. W. M. (1954), "The Cross-Cultural Method," in *Handbook of Social Psychology,* Gardner Lindzey, ed. Reading, Mass.: Addison-Wesley.

Whyte, W. F. (1962), "Measuring Entrepreneurial Attitudes to Work Cross-Culturally." Unpublished Working Paper. Cornell University School of Industrial Relations.

Williams, L. K. (1962), "Development of a Risk-Taking Scale." Unpublished Working Paper. Cornell University School of Industrial Relations.

Wursten, H. (1960), "Story Completions: Madeline Thomas Stories and Similar Methods," in *Projective Techniques with Children,* A. I. Rabin and M. R. Haworth, eds. New York: Grune and Stratton, 192–209.

Index